ĐÀN BÀ THƠ

Đàn bà thơ, đón gió mưa
Lá vương sợi nhớ hương thừa mặn môi
Nghịch mùa chiếc lá tình phơi
Tím mơ khép lại, lùa trôi nắng ngày

Phố buồn không uống mà say
Nâng ly chạm nhớ, rót đầy ý thơ
Đàn bà bước ngắn bước ngơ
Phấn thừa hương cũ sương mờ mịt giăng
......
Trời chiều tím ngọn Bằng lăng
Tình em nhuộm tím vầng trăng trời chiều.

07.10.2017

TIẾNG THẠCH SÙNG

Thạch sùng treo ngược cuộc đời trên tấm vách
Mắt lim dim vờ khép
Tiếc thời gian chật
Tiếc lòng người chật
Tiếc ánh nhìn chật

Thạch sùng đêm đêm tắc lưỡi với đời
Ngẫm chữ vô thường
Triệu người biết, vạn người đọc, trăm người nghe
Hỏi:
Mấy người hiểu?

Nằm trong căn phòng chật
Giàu cô đơn
Giàu nước mắt
Giàu suy tưởng
Một chiếc bóng in lồng trong tâm tưởng
Gà gáy, sương tan,... bóng khuất

Chiếc đèn dầu tâm thức leo lét
Thạch sùng thôi tắc lưỡi
Chuyến đò trôi xuôi
Vô thường gõ cửa.

01.11.2017

Mục lục

1. Sài Gòn nay	14
2. Ta trọ nhà ta	15
3. Lạc nhịp quê hương	16
4. Sương trắng sa	18
5. Dòng sông kỉ niệm	19
6. Vén trời Paris	20
7. Ngày chớm xanh	22
8. Đêm trắng đêm	23
9. Khi viết cong ngòi	24
10. Da vàng trên đất khách	25
11. Dải lụa vàng	26
12. Giấc mơ đàn bà	27
13. Nứt nụ đoá vô ưu	28
14. Hoa bất tử	30
15. Rồi đây tôi đi biển	32
16. Giếng & gầu	34
17. Câu kinh chín mùa	35
18. Giấc mơ em	37
19. Dậy mùa	38
20. Bàn tay độ lượng	39
21. Ngả nón nghiêng vành	40
22. Búp non cành nhà	41

23. Hoá thạch ngôn ngữ	42
24. Vàng đồng lúa chín	44
25. Cầu tre lắt lẻo	45
26. Việt Nam - đất nước tôi	46
27. Bẻ khoá quay về	48
28. Bóng câu chìm nổi	50
29. Paris vàng	52
30. Đôi khi	53
31. Xoá vết màu rêu	54
32. Vẽ đời mộng mị	55
33. Cơn đau không người gánh	56
34. Cơn đau tá túc	58
35. Vui sống	59
36. Cành mềm xa tổ	60
37. Yêu lời nắng thổi	62
38. Bán nỗi buồn	63
39. Nhặt trời độ lượng	64
40. Nếu em là cỏ dại	66
41. Nắng hẹn mai sẽ lên	67
42. Đêm trắng Paris	68
43. Tiếng thở dài	69
44. Ngọn đèn mẫu tử	70
45. Ủ thóc xanh bồ	72
46. Trăng thu dậy mùa	73
47. Em của ngày hôm nay	74
48. Phận chảo xoong	77

49. Xin được gieo ân điển	78
50. Trở giấc mùa rêu	79
51. Tiễn ba lần cuối	80
52. Hoa nở mùa sau	82
53. Khuyết mùa Vu lan	84
54. Gió thổi phận lồng	85
55. Vãng sanh tịnh độ	86
56. Giấc mơ qua	87
57. Mấy ai?	88
58. Người đàn bà (2)	89
59. Nhìn	90
60. Lời thì thầm	91
61. Cho em được một lần	92
62. Xin đừng bước vội	94
63. Mùa thương có về	95
64. Xuân về trong hơi thở	96
65. Còn lời trăm năm	97
66. Sâu & lá	98
67. Cơn say lại	99
68. Soi bóng	100
69. Đàn bà thơ	101
70. Tiếng thạch sùng	102

Liên lạc Tác giả
Đặng Thị Lụa
luadang1976@yahoo.com.vn

Liên lạc Nhà xuất bản
Nhân Ảnh
han.le3359@gmail.com
(408) 722-5626

www.ingramcontent.com/pod-product-compliance
Lightning Source LLC
Chambersburg PA
CBHW052101280426
43673CB00069B/11

Short Stories for Teen Girls

Life-Changing Tales With Deep Meaning for Modern Teenagers

Grace Parker

© Copyright 2025 – Grace Parker – All rights reserved

The content within this book may not be reproduced, duplicated, or transmitted without direct written permission from the author or the publisher.

Under no circumstances will any blame or legal responsibility be held against the publisher, or author, for any damages, reparation, or monetary loss due to the information contained within this book, either directly or indirectly.

Legal Notice

This book is copyright protected. This book is only for personal use. You cannot amend, distribute, sell, use, quote, or paraphrase any part, or the content within this book, without the consent of the author-publisher.

Disclaimer Notice

Please note that the information contained within this document is for educational and entertainment purposes only. All effort has been executed to present accurate, up-to-date, and reliable, complete information. No warranties of any kind are declared or implied. Readers acknowledge that the author is not engaging in the rendering of legal, financial, medical, or professional advice.

Table of Content

About Me and Why I Wrote This Book 4

Introduction 6

Authenticity Beats Popularity 8

Perfection Is an Illusion 13

Your Uniqueness Is Your Superpower 18

Comparison Steals Joy 24

Beauty Is So Much More Than Skin Deep 30

Courage Isn't the Absence of Fear 37

Failure Is Your Best Teacher 44

Your Comfort Zone Is Where Dreams Go to Die 52

Vulnerability Is Real Strength 61

Change Is the Only Constant 69

True Friendship Shows Up in the Storm 78

Words Can Hurt or Heal 87

Judging Is Easy, Understanding Takes Courage 96

Forgiveness Frees You, Not Just Them 105

Your Family Roots Are Hidden Treasure 114

Your Inner Voice Always Knows the Truth 123

Someone Else's Success Isn't Your Failure 132

Small Choices Build Your Big Future 141

Giving Enriches More Than Receiving 150

Your Values Are Your Compass 160

A Final Note 170

About Me and Why I Wrote This Book

I didn't plan to write this book. I planned to help my two teenage daughters.

Like many parents, I watched my girls navigate a world that felt more complicated than anything I'd experienced at their age. The pressure to be perfect. The constant comparison on social media. The fear of not being enough. They were struggling, and despite all my love and good intentions, I didn't always know how to help.

Traditional advice wasn't working. When I tried to talk directly about these issues, I was met with eye rolls or the dreaded "You don't understand, Mom." And maybe they were right. Their teenage experience was different from mine. But the core struggles, the fundamental questions of identity and worth and belonging, those were universal.

So I tried something different. I started writing stories.

Not advice or lectures, but real narratives about girls facing real challenges. Stories that showed instead of told. Stories where characters discovered life lessons through their own experiences, not through adults telling them what to think.

I shared the first story with my oldest daughter on a night she was feeling particularly low. She read it quietly, then looked up at me with tears in her eyes. "This is exactly how I feel," she said. "Can you write another one?"

So I did. Then another. And another.

Soon, both my girls were asking me to write more. They started sharing the stories with their friends. Those friends asked for copies. I found myself writing stories about the challenges these girls brought to me. Body image. Academic pressure. Toxic relationships. Fear of failure.

These stories became our bridge. A way to talk about hard things without the awkwardness of direct advice. A way for them to see themselves in characters who struggled, grew, and found their way forward.

What started as a mother trying to connect with her daughters became something bigger. These twenty stories represent conversations with my girls, insights from their experiences, and lessons I wish someone had shared with me when I was sixteen.

I wrote this book for my daughters. But I'm sharing it with yours.

Because every teenage girl deserves to know she's not alone in her struggles. That her feelings are valid. That growth is possible. That she has everything she needs inside her to navigate whatever challenges come her way.

These stories won't solve every problem. But they might spark a conversation. They might offer a new perspective. They might help a girl see herself, her worth, and her potential in a new light.

And sometimes, that's exactly what makes the difference.

Grace lives with her family and continues to write stories that bridge the gap between the teenage experience and the wisdom that comes with surviving it. This is her first book, but not her last conversation with the girls who need to hear these messages.

Introduction

If you're reading this, you're probably a teenage girl trying to figure things out. Or maybe you're a parent who wants to understand what your daughter is going through. Either way, welcome.

This book isn't going to tell you what to do. It's not going to lecture you about how to live your life or who to be. You've probably had enough of that already.

Instead, this is a collection of twenty stories about girls just like you. Girls facing real challenges. Girls making mistakes, learning lessons, and figuring out who they are. Some of these stories might feel like they were written about you. Others might show you a perspective you've never considered. That's the point.

Each story explores a life lesson, something I believe every teenage girl should know. But these lessons aren't told to you, they're shown through characters who discover them on their own journey. Because that's how real growth happens. Not through someone else's advice, but through your own experience and reflection.

At the end of each story, you'll find a "Reflect & Grow" section with questions to think about. You don't have to answer them. You don't have to share them with anyone. But I encourage you to sit with them. To think about how the story connects to your own life. That's where the real magic happens.

How to Use This Book

You don't have to read these stories in order. If you're struggling with friendship drama, jump to "True Friendship Shows Up in the Storm." If you're dealing with comparison and social media, "Comparison Steals Joy" might speak to you. If you just finished a difficult experience and need perspective, "Failure Is Your Best Teacher" could help. You can read one story and put the book down for a month. You can read all twenty in one sitting. You can share stories with friends or keep them private. There's no right way to do this.

This book is yours. Use it however it serves you best.

A Note to Parents

If you're reading this because you bought the book for your daughter, thank you. These stories might open doors to conversations you've been wanting to have. But here's my advice: let her read them first. Let her come to you if she wants to talk about them. Don't use these stories as teaching moments or springboards for lectures. Just let them be what they are, stories that might help her see herself and her challenges in a new light.

To Every Girl Reading This

You're navigating one of the hardest periods of human development in one of the most complicated times in history. You're dealing with pressures and challenges that didn't exist even ten years ago. And you're doing it while your brain is still developing, your body is changing, and you're trying to figure out who you are.

That's incredibly hard. And you're doing better than you think.

These stories won't solve all your problems. They won't make the hard things easy. But they might help you feel less alone. They might give you a new way to think about a challenge you're facing. They might remind you that growth is possible, that mistakes are normal, and that you have everything you need inside you to navigate whatever comes next.

You've got this. Even when it doesn't feel like it.

Now, let's dive into some stories.

Grace.

Authenticity Beats Popularity

Maya stared at her phone screen, her thumb hovering over the "post" button. The selfie looked perfect, at least, it looked like what everyone else was posting. The angle. The filter. The casual-but-not-too-casual smile. Everything calculated to get likes.

But something felt wrong.

"You coming?" her best friend Zoe called from the kitchen. "Your mom made those amazing cookies!"

Maya quickly locked her phone and shoved it in her pocket. "Yeah, coming!"

At the kitchen table, Zoe was already on her third cookie, crumbs scattered across her vintage band t-shirt. Maya's mom laughed at something Zoe said, her eyes crinkling at the corners.

"So, Maya," Zoe said between bites, "are you still sitting with us at lunch tomorrow, or are you gonna sit with the Instagram crew again?"

There it was. The question Maya had been dreading.

Two weeks ago, Madison Clarke (yes, *the* Madison Clarke, with her perfect hair and 5,000 followers) had invited Maya to sit at her table. Just once, Madison said. But once turned into twice, and twice turned into every day.

"I don't know what you mean by 'Instagram crew,'" Maya said, avoiding Zoe's eyes.

"Come on, Maya. They literally spend the entire lunch period taking photos of their food and themselves. Do they even eat?"

Maya felt her cheeks burn. "They're not that bad. Madison's actually really nice once you get to know her."

"Is she?" Zoe's voice was quiet now, and that somehow made it worse. "Because from where I'm sitting, it looks like you're becoming someone else to fit in with them."

"That's not fair!"

"Isn't it?" Zoe stood up, brushing crumbs off her shirt. "You used to wear those weird vintage scarves you loved. You used to talk about books and art. Now you're worried about the perfect selfie and whether your outfit is 'aesthetic' enough."

Maya wanted to argue, but the words stuck in her throat. Because deep down, she knew Zoe was right.

The next day at lunch, Maya found herself at Madison's table again. The conversation flowed around her like water around a stone. Fashion brands she'd never heard of, drama with people she barely knew, the eternal question of which filter made you look most "natural."

"Oh my God, Maya, you're so quiet today!" Madison said, tilting her head with practiced concern. "Is everything okay?"

"Yeah, I'm fine."

"Good! Because I need your opinion." Madison held up her phone. "Which photo should I post? This one or this one? They're literally identical, but like, the vibe is different, you know?"

Maya looked at the two nearly identical photos. In both, Madison looked stunning. Perfect. Untouchable.

"They're both great," Maya said automatically.

"Ugh, you're no help!" Madison laughed, but there was an edge to it. "Hey, speaking of posts, I saw you're still following that weird girl. What's her name? Zoe? The one with the thrift store clothes?"

Maya's stomach tightened. "She's my best friend."

"Oh, I know, I know! I'm not saying unfollow her or anything. Just... maybe don't, like, comment on her posts too much? It's kind of off-brand for you now."

"Off-brand?" The word tasted bitter.

"You know what I mean. You're sitting with us now. People notice who you associate with." Madison's smile was sweet, but her eyes were calculating. "I'm just trying to help you. That's what friends do, right?"

That afternoon, Maya sat in art class, staring at a blank canvas. Mrs. Patterson had given them a simple assignment: paint something that represents who you are.

Maya's brush hovered over the palette. Who was she? The girl who wore vintage scarves and read poetry? Or the girl who knew the perfect Instagram caption and the right filter for every occasion?

Her phone buzzed. A text from Zoe: *Miss you. Found a new bookstore downtown. Thought you'd want to check it out this weekend.*

Then another buzz. Madison: *Emergency! Need you to take photos of me after school. The lighting is PERFECT right now.*

Maya looked at both messages. Then she looked at her blank canvas.

Slowly, she began to paint.

The next day at lunch, Maya walked into the cafeteria wearing her grandmother's vintage scarf, the one with the yellow flowers she hadn't worn in weeks. Her heart pounded as she passed Madison's table.

"Maya! Over here!" Madison called, waving.

Maya took a deep breath and kept walking. She made her way to the corner table where Zoe sat alone, reading a book with a cracked spine.

Zoe looked up, surprise flickering across her face. "Hey."

"Hey." Maya set down her tray and sat. "So, about that bookstore..."

"You're seriously ditching us?" Madison's voice cut through the cafeteria noise. She had walked over, her phone in one hand, her perfect eyebrows raised. "After everything?"

Maya looked up at her. "I'm not ditching anyone. I'm just... sitting with my actual friend."

"Your 'actual friend'?" Madison laughed, but it sounded forced. "Maya, I was trying to help you. You could have been popular. You could have mattered."

"I already matter," Maya said quietly. "I just forgot that for a while."

Madison stared at her for a long moment, her phone still in her hand, probably ready to document this moment for her followers. Then she shrugged. "Whatever. Your loss."

As Madison walked away, Maya felt something lift from her chest, something heavy she hadn't realized she'd been carrying.

"That was brave," Zoe said softly.

"That was terrifying," Maya corrected, but she was smiling. "I missed this. I missed us."

"I missed you too." Zoe grinned. "The real you, not the filtered version."

Maya laughed, and it felt genuine for the first time in weeks. "Yeah, well, the real me is kind of a mess."

"The real you is perfect," Zoe said. "Messy and all."

That night, Maya sat on her bed, looking at the selfie she'd almost posted weeks ago. The one with the perfect angle and the perfect filter. The one that looked like everyone else.

She deleted it.

Instead, she posted a photo Zoe had taken of her in art class, paint on her hands, her grandmother's scarf around her neck, laughing at something off-camera. The caption was simple: *Being myself is way more fun than being perfect.*

The likes came slowly, nowhere near what Madison's posts got. But the comments were different. Real friends. Real reactions. Real connections.

And that, Maya realized, was worth more than a thousand followers.

Reflect & Grow

Questions for you:

- *Have you ever changed who you are to fit in with a certain group? How did it make you feel?*
- *What does "authenticity" mean to you? What parts of yourself do you sometimes hide?*
- *Who are the people in your life who love you for who you really are, not who you pretend to be?*
- *What's one thing you could do this week to be more authentically yourself, even if it feels scary?*

Remember: Popularity is temporary, but authenticity is forever. The right people will love you for who you truly are, and those are the only people who matter.

Perfection Is an Illusion

Sophie Reed had never gotten a B in her life. Not once. Not ever. She stared at the algebra test on her desk, the red "B+" circled at the top like a scar. Her hands trembled as she shoved the paper into her backpack before anyone could see it.

"How'd you do?" her friend Emma asked, leaning over.

"Fine," Sophie said quickly. "The usual."

Emma grinned. "Of course you did. You're like, genetically incapable of getting anything less than an A."

Sophie forced a smile, but inside, panic clawed at her chest. This wasn't supposed to happen. Perfect Sophie Reed didn't get B's. Perfect Sophie Reed was valedictorian material, Harvard-bound, the girl who had it all together.

Except she didn't. Not anymore.

At home, Sophie sat at her desk, the test hidden at the bottom of her backpack like evidence of a crime. Her bedroom was exactly how people expected it to be. Neat. Organized. Color-coded binders lined up on her shelf. A corkboard covered with perfectly arranged photos, achievement certificates, and a printed college prep timeline.

Her phone buzzed. A text from her mom: *How was the algebra test? I'm sure you aced it as always! So proud of you, sweetie.*

Sophie's stomach twisted. She typed back: *It went well!* Then she added a smiley face and hit send.

Lying to her mom felt awful, but telling the truth felt impossible. Her parents had framed every report card she'd ever gotten. They introduced her to their friends as "our little overachiever." Her dad's favorite joke was, "Sophie's middle name should be 'Perfect.'"

What would they say if they knew the truth? That their perfect daughter was cracking under the pressure?

The next day in English class, Mrs. Chen announced a creative writing assignment. "I want you to write about a time you failed at something and what you learned from it."

Sophie's pen froze over her notebook. Failed? She didn't fail. That was the whole point.

Around her, other students were already scribbling ideas. Emma leaned over and whispered, "I'm writing about that time I tried out for the soccer team and totally embarrassed myself. What about you?"

"I... I don't know yet," Sophie said.

The truth was, she couldn't think of a single failure she was willing to share. Because failures weren't supposed to exist in Sophie Reed's perfect world.

That afternoon, Sophie found herself in the art room during free period. She rarely came here. Art was messy, unpredictable, and worst of all, subjective. There was no rubric for "perfect" in art.

But today, she needed to escape.

"Hey, Sophie!" A girl named Mia looked up from her canvas, paintbrush in hand. Her hands were covered in different colors, and there was a smear of blue on her cheek. "Didn't know you did art."

"I don't, really. Just... needed a quiet place to think."

"Well, you picked the wrong room for quiet," Mia laughed. "But you're welcome to stay. Want to try painting something?"

Sophie looked at the blank canvases stacked in the corner. Something about their emptiness felt both terrifying and liberating. "I wouldn't even know where to start. I'm not good at art."

"So?" Mia shrugged. "Neither was I when I started. That's kind of the point. You just... try stuff and see what happens."

"But what if it turns out terrible?"

"Then it turns out terrible." Mia grinned. "It's not the end of the world, you know. Sometimes terrible is more interesting than perfect anyway."

Sophie picked up a brush hesitantly. Her hand shook slightly as she dipped it in paint. What color? What should she paint? What if...

"You're thinking too much," Mia said gently. "Just put the brush on the canvas and see what happens."

Sophie took a breath and made a single blue stroke across the canvas. It wasn't elegant. It wasn't planned. It was just... there.

And somehow, that felt okay.

Over the next week, Sophie kept going back to the art room. Her painting was a mess, honestly. Random colors, no clear subject, no technique. But something about creating something imperfect felt like exhaling after holding her breath for years.

Then came the day she'd been dreading. Parent-teacher conferences.

Sophie sat in the hallway outside the math classroom, her heart racing. Through the door, she could hear Mr. Harrison talking to her parents.

"Sophie is an exceptional student," he was saying. "But I've noticed she seems very stressed lately. That last test, she got a B+, which is still excellent, but she seemed devastated by it."

There was a pause. Then her mom's voice, concerned. "A B+? She told us she did well. She always does well."

"That's just it, Mrs. Reed. A B+ *is* doing well. But Sophie seems to believe anything less than perfect is failure. I'm worried about the pressure she's putting on herself."

Sophie's dad spoke up. "We've never pressured her to be perfect. We just want her to do her best."

"I understand," Mr. Harrison said. "But sometimes, kids don't hear 'do your best.' They hear 'be the best.' And there's a big difference."

Sophie felt tears burning in her eyes. She stood up and pushed through the door.

"Sophie!" Her mom looked surprised. "Honey, we were just..."

"I'm sorry," Sophie said, her voice cracking. "I'm sorry I got a B. I'm sorry I'm not perfect. I'm sorry I lied about the test. I just... I didn't want to disappoint you."

Her parents exchanged a look. Then her mom stood up and pulled Sophie into a hug.

"Sweetheart, you could never disappoint us. Never."

"But you're always so proud of my grades. You always tell everyone how perfect I am. I thought..."

"We're proud of *you*," her dad said, standing up too. "Not your grades. You. The person you are."

"But I'm not perfect," Sophie whispered. "I'm really, really not perfect."

"Good," her mom said, pulling back to look at her. "Because perfect is boring. And impossible. And honestly, kind of sad."

Sophie blinked. "What?"

"Sophie, do you know what I regret most about my teenage years?" her mom asked. "I spent so much time trying to be perfect that I forgot to actually enjoy being young. I want more for you than that."

Mr. Harrison spoke up gently. "Sophie, you're one of my best students. But I'd rather see you learn and grow and sometimes struggle than watch you slowly burn out trying to be flawless. Making mistakes is how we learn. It's how we become better."

That night, Sophie sat in her room, looking at her corkboard. All those certificates. All those perfect report cards. All that proof that she was good enough.

But was she really? Or was she just... perfect on paper?

She took down the corkboard and pulled out the painting she'd made in art class. It was messy. Imperfect. Kind of ugly, honestly.

But it was real. It was hers. And she'd made it without fear.

Sophie pinned the painting to her wall, right above her desk where the corkboard used to be. Then she pulled out her English assignment and began to write. *"The time I failed was actually the time I learned the most important lesson of my life. I got a B+ on an algebra test, and I thought my world was ending. But it wasn't ending. It was actually beginning..."* For the first time in years, Sophie Reed wasn't trying to write the perfect essay. She was just trying to write the truth. And somehow, that felt more perfect than anything she'd ever done.

Reflect & Grow

Questions for you:

- *What does "perfect" mean to you? Who decides what perfect is?*
- *When was the last time you made a mistake? What did you learn from it?*
- *Are you harder on yourself than you would be on a friend in the same situation? Why?*
- *What would you do differently if you weren't afraid of being imperfect?*

Remember: Perfection is an illusion that keeps you from growing. Your mistakes, your struggles, and your imperfections are what make you interesting, real, and ultimately, stronger. The goal isn't to be perfect. The goal is to be authentically, beautifully, messily yourself.

Your Uniqueness Is Your Superpower

P riya Sharma hated the first day of school. Not because of new classes or homework or early mornings. She hated it because of the same question she got every single year.

"Wait, so where are you *really* from?"

She was from Michigan. Born and raised. But people never seemed satisfied with that answer when they looked at her brown skin and heard her "unusual" name.

"Michigan," Priya said to the girl sitting next to her in homeroom, already exhausted and it wasn't even 9 AM.

"No, I mean, like, originally. What's your background?"

"My parents are from India. I'm from here."

The girl nodded like she'd solved a puzzle. "Oh, that's so cool! I love Indian food. Do you speak Indian?"

Priya bit back the urge to explain that "Indian" wasn't a language. "Hindi. A little. My grandma speaks it more than I do."

"That's amazing! You're so lucky to be bilingual."

Lucky. Right. Lucky to be the girl who brought "weird" lunches to school. Lucky to be asked to explain her culture like she was a walking encyclopedia. Lucky to never quite fit in anywhere, too American for her relatives in India, too Indian for some of her classmates here.

At lunch, Priya sat with her friend group, the same girls she'd known since middle school. They were nice enough, but sometimes Priya felt like she was playing a part. The quirky ethnic friend. The one who added "diversity" to their Instagram photos.

"Oh my God, Priya, what is that?" Jessica pointed at Priya's lunch. "It smells so… strong."

Priya looked down at her container of aloo gobi, the cauliflower and potato dish her mom had packed. At home, it was comfort food. Here, it was just another thing that made her different.

"It's just vegetables," Priya said quietly, suddenly wishing she'd asked for a boring sandwich instead.

"It looks good!" Emma said, too enthusiastically. "Very authentic."

There was that word again. Authentic. Like Priya's existence was a cultural exhibit.

After school, Priya went to the community center for the first meeting of the year for Creative Writing Club. It was the only place she felt like she could breathe, where words mattered more than where you came from.

Except this year, there was a new club advisor. Ms. Rodriguez, a young teacher with kind eyes and a notebook covered in colorful stickers.

"Alright, everyone," Ms. Rodriguez said, "this year, we're going to focus on writing what we know. Your unique experiences, your specific lens on the world. Because that's what makes writing powerful. Not when we all try to sound the same, but when we dare to sound like ourselves."

She looked around the room. "I want each of you to write about something that makes you different. Something you maybe try to hide or downplay. And I want you to write it like it's your superpower, not your weakness."

Priya's stomach clenched. Write about being different? She spent most of her energy trying *not* to be different.

That night, Priya sat at her desk, staring at a blank document. What made her different? Everything. Nothing. Too much.

Her phone buzzed. A text from Jessica: *OMG look at this Bollywood dance video! Made me think of you!*

Priya sighed. Jessica meant well, but it was exhausting being reduced to a stereotype. Not every Indian person loved Bollywood or knew how to dance or ate curry every day or...

Wait.

Priya started typing, her fingers flying across the keyboard.

"People think they know me because they can see my skin and hear my name. They think they've got me figured out. Indian girl. Must love spicy food. Must be good at math. Must have strict parents. Must, must, must.

But here's what they don't know: I hate math. My favorite food is actually pizza. My parents let me make my own choices. I listen to punk rock, not just Bollywood music. I'm terrible at dancing. I say 'like' too much and I've never worn a sari in my life.

I'm Indian and American and neither and both. I'm Priya Sharma from Michigan who happens to have roots in Gujarat. I contain multitudes, just like everyone else. But somehow, I'm the only one who has to constantly explain myself.

And honestly? I'm tired of it."

Priya stopped, her heart pounding. She'd never written anything that honest before.

At the next writing club meeting, Ms. Rodriguez asked for volunteers to share their work. Priya's hand stayed firmly on her lap. No way was she reading that out loud.

But then Marcus, a quiet kid who usually sat in the back, raised his hand. He walked to the front and read a piece about being the only Black kid in his Advanced Physics class, about teachers being surprised by his intelligence, about constantly having to prove himself.

When he finished, the room was silent. Then someone started clapping, and everyone joined in.

"Thank you, Marcus," Ms. Rodriguez said softly. "That took courage."

Marcus sat down, and for the first time since Priya had known him, he was smiling. Really smiling. Like he'd put down something heavy he'd been carrying.

Priya's hand went up before she could stop herself.

Walking to the front of the room felt like walking through water. Priya's voice shook as she started reading, but with each word, something shifted. The words weren't just on the page anymore. They were in the room, in the air, real and true and hers.

When she finished, there was silence. Priya's cheeks burned. She'd made a mistake. She'd said too much. She'd...

"Yes," someone said. It was Angela, a Korean American girl Priya had never really talked to. "Yes. Exactly that."

"I feel that way too," another voice said. "About being Latina. About people thinking they know my whole story."

"About being adopted," someone else added. "About not looking like my family."

Suddenly, everyone was talking, sharing, connecting. All the things that made them different, that made them feel alone, were actually the things that brought them together.

Ms. Rodriguez caught Priya's eye and smiled. "See? Your uniqueness isn't something to hide. It's your voice. And the world needs to hear it."

The next day at lunch, Priya unpacked her aloo gobi without hesitation. When Jessica wrinkled her nose, Priya didn't apologize or explain.

"It's cauliflower and potatoes," she said simply. "My mom makes it really well. Want to try some?"

Jessica hesitated, then nodded. She took a small bite, and her eyebrows went up. "Oh. That's actually really good."

"Yeah," Priya said. "It is."

Emma leaned over. "Hey, I've been wanting to ask you something. Not in a weird way, I promise. But... what's it like? Being Indian American? I realized I've known you for years and I've never really asked. Like, actually asked to understand, not just to be nosy."

Priya looked at Emma, really looked at her. There was genuine curiosity there, not the performative kind. Not the "you're so exotic" kind. Just... wanting to know.

"It's complicated," Priya said. "But it's also pretty cool. I can switch between languages. I get two sets of holidays. I understand references from both Bollywood movies and American TV shows. I'm like... culturally bilingual."

"That *is* cool," Emma said. "I never thought about it that way."

"Yeah," Priya said, feeling something unfold in her chest. Pride, maybe. Or just acceptance. "Neither did I. But I'm starting to."

That weekend, Priya wore a kurta to the mall, the embroidered Indian tunic her grandmother had sent for her birthday. She'd been keeping it in her closet, too nervous to wear it outside the house.

But today, walking through the food court in her kurta and jeans, Priya felt different. Not invisible. Not trying to blend in. Just... herself.

A little girl tugged on her mother's sleeve. "Mommy, look at her shirt! It's so pretty!"

The mother smiled apologetically at Priya, but Priya smiled back. "Thank you," she said to the little girl. "My grandma picked it out for me."

"It's beautiful," the girl said, her eyes wide.

And in that moment, Priya realized something. Her uniqueness wasn't something to overcome or hide or apologize for. It was her story. Her voice. Her superpower.

And she was finally ready to own it.

Reflect & Grow

Questions for you:

- *What makes you different from the people around you? How do you feel about those differences?*
- *Have you ever hidden parts of yourself to fit in? What would it feel like to stop hiding?*
- *What's something unique about your background, your family, or your interests that you could celebrate instead of downplay?*
- *How can you use your unique perspective to connect with others instead of feeling isolated by it?*

Remember: The things that make you different are not flaws to fix. They are colors in your unique painting, notes in your specific song. Your perspective, shaped by your experiences and background, is something no one else can offer. That's not a weakness. That's your superpower.

Comparison Steals Joy

Lily Chen refreshed her Instagram feed for the third time in five minutes.

There it was again. Another post from Natasha Williams. This time, Natasha was at the beach, her perfect smile gleaming in the sunset, her caption reading: *Best summer ever! So grateful for this amazing life!*

Lily looked at her own life. She was sitting on her worn couch in her small apartment, wearing pajamas at 2 PM, scrolling through other people's highlight reels while her own summer felt like a lowlight reel.

Her mom walked by with a laundry basket. "Lily, honey, did you practice your violin today?"

"Not yet," Lily muttered, still staring at her phone.

She scrolled down. There was Ashley Kim, posing with her debate team trophy. Then Marcus from school, showing off his new car. Then Jennifer Lopez (wait, why was she following Jennifer Lopez?), looking flawless at some red carpet event.

Everyone's life looked perfect. Everyone except hers.

The violin had been Lily's thing since she was seven. She was good at it, really good. Her teacher said she had natural talent, that rare combination of technical skill and emotional depth.

But lately, playing felt different. Every time Lily picked up her bow, she thought about Sarah Zhang, the violinist in her youth orchestra who always got the solos. Sarah, who had performed at Carnegie Hall last year. Sarah, whose parents could afford the expensive summer music camps that Lily's family couldn't.

Lily opened YouTube and searched for Sarah's Carnegie Hall performance. She watched it once, then twice, each viewing making her chest feel tighter.

Sarah was incredible. Flawless technique. Perfect posture. The comments were full of praise. "Prodigy!" "Future star!" "Absolutely breathtaking!"

Lily closed her laptop and looked at her violin case in the corner. What was the point? She'd never be that good. She'd never play Carnegie Hall. She'd never be Sarah Zhang.

At her next violin lesson, Lily's teacher, Mrs. Patterson, noticed immediately.

"You're distracted today," Mrs. Patterson said gently. "Where's your mind?"

Lily shrugged. "I don't know. I guess I'm just wondering if I'm good enough. Like, really good enough."

"Good enough for what?"

"For... anything. To be special. To matter." Lily's voice cracked. "There are so many people better than me. I saw Sarah Zhang's performance at Carnegie Hall and I just... I'll never be that good."

Mrs. Patterson set down her own violin and sat next to Lily. "Can I tell you a secret? I spent my entire twenties comparing myself to other violinists. Every performance, every recording, every competition. I was never the best, and it ate me alive."

"But you're amazing," Lily protested.

"Thank you. But here's what I learned too late. Comparison is a thief. It steals your joy, your progress, and worst of all, it steals your unique voice." Mrs. Patterson picked up Lily's violin and handed it to her. "Sarah Zhang plays like Sarah Zhang. But you play like Lily Chen. And the world needs both."

"But her technique..."

"Is hers. Not yours. Lily, when you play, you bring something to the music that Sarah never could. Your experiences, your emotions, your perspective. That's not less than. It's just different. And different is valuable."

Lily looked down at her violin. "I used to love playing. Now I just feel like I'm not good enough."

"That's because you're measuring yourself against someone else's ruler. Stop looking at Sarah's journey and focus on your own."

That night, Lily did something radical. She deleted Instagram from her phone.

Not forever, she told herself. Just for a while. Just to see what it felt like to not know what everyone else was doing every second of every day.

The first day was weird. She reached for her phone constantly, muscle memory pulling her to an app that wasn't there anymore. But by day three, something shifted.

Without the constant stream of other people's achievements, Lily noticed things she'd been missing. The way the light came through her window in the morning. The way her little sister laughed at cartoons. The way her mom hummed while cooking dinner.

Small things. Ordinary things. Things that didn't look impressive on social media but felt good in real life.

On Saturday, Lily picked up her violin without thinking about Sarah Zhang or Carnegie Hall or being the best. She just played. A simple piece she'd known since childhood, nothing fancy or impressive.

But something was different. The music felt like hers again. Not perfect, but honest. Not flawless, but real.

Her little sister, Emma, wandered into the room and sat on the floor, listening. When Lily finished, Emma clapped enthusiastically.

"That was so pretty, Lily!"

"Thanks, Em. It's just a simple song though."

"I don't care. It made me happy." Emma smiled. "When you play, it makes the whole house feel nicer."

Lily blinked back sudden tears. When had she stopped noticing that? When had making her little sister happy become less important than comparing herself to some girl she'd never even met?

At youth orchestra rehearsal the next week, Sarah Zhang was there, preparing for another competition. She looked stressed, snapping at her stand partner, obsessively checking her phone between pieces.

During break, Lily gathered her courage and walked over. "Hey, Sarah. I just wanted to say, I saw your Carnegie Hall performance online. It was really beautiful."

Sarah looked up, surprised. "Oh. Thanks." Then she sighed. "Honestly? I've watched that video like a hundred times. All I can see are the mistakes."

"Mistakes? It sounded perfect to me."

"There were three tiny intonation issues in the second movement. My bow hold was off in the cadenza. And..." Sarah laughed bitterly, "my mom's friend's daughter just got accepted to Juilliard at fifteen. Fifteen. I'm seventeen and I haven't even applied yet."

Lily stared at her. Sarah Zhang, the girl she'd been envying for months, was comparing herself to someone else too. The cycle never ended.

"Can I tell you something my teacher told me?" Lily said. "Comparison is a thief. It steals your joy."

Sarah was quiet for a moment. Then she smiled, a real smile this time, not the performative kind. "Your teacher sounds smart."

"She is." Lily smiled back. "Hey, want to grab coffee after rehearsal? Not to talk about music or competitions or college. Just... to hang out?"

"Yeah," Sarah said, looking relieved. "I'd really like that."

That night, Lily reinstalled Instagram. But this time, she did something different. Instead of mindlessly scrolling, she posted a video of herself playing violin. Not her best performance. Not perfectly lit or edited. Just her, in her room, playing a piece she loved.

The caption was simple: *Learning to enjoy the music instead of chasing perfection. Learning to run my own race.*

The likes came slowly. Twenty. Thirty. Nothing compared to the hundreds that Natasha's beach photos got.

But then the comments started.

This is so real. Thank you for sharing.

I needed to hear this today.

Your playing is beautiful. Don't ever stop.

And one comment from a username she didn't recognize: *Comparison is the thief of joy. Keep being you.*

Lily smiled. Maybe that was the secret. Maybe joy wasn't found in being better than everyone else. Maybe it was found in being fully, authentically yourself. In running your own race at your own pace. In celebrating your own small victories instead of measuring them against someone else's highlight reel.

She picked up her violin and played. Not for Carnegie Hall. Not for Instagram. Not to be better than Sarah Zhang.

Just for herself. Just for the joy of it.

And somehow, that was enough.

Reflect & Grow

Questions for you:

- *Who do you compare yourself to most often? On social media? In real life? How does that comparison make you feel?*
- *What would your life look like if you spent less time looking at what others are doing and more time enjoying what you're doing?*
- *What's something you used to love that comparison has stolen the joy from? How can you reclaim it?*
- *What makes your journey unique? What do you bring to the world that no one else can?*

Remember: Someone else's success is not your failure. Someone else's highlight reel is not your behind-the-scenes. You are not running their race. You're running yours. And your race, with all its unique challenges and victories, is exactly where you're supposed to be. Comparison will always leave you feeling empty. But gratitude for your own journey? That's where real joy lives.

Beauty Is So Much More Than Skin Deep

Rachel Thompson stood in front of her bathroom mirror, pulling at the skin on her face, wishing she could rearrange it into something prettier.

Her nose was too big. Her eyes were too small. Her hair was too frizzy. Her skin had that one stupid pimple that seemed to glow like a beacon. And don't even get her started on her body.

She grabbed her phone and opened TikTok, where girls with perfect skin and perfect hair and perfect everything showed off their "natural beauty" routines that somehow required twenty different products and Ring lights.

Rachel's older sister, Nicole, knocked on the bathroom door. "Rach, you've been in there for like an hour. I need to get ready too."

"Just a minute," Rachel called back, applying another layer of concealer to that stupid pimple.

When she finally opened the door, Nicole took one look at her and frowned. "Why are you wearing so much makeup? We're just going to the community center."

"I'm not wearing that much."

"Rachel, I can barely see your face under all that foundation."

"Well, maybe that's the point," Rachel snapped, pushing past her sister.

At the community center, Rachel was volunteering for their summer program, helping organize activities for elementary school kids. It was something she did every year, mostly because it looked good on college applications, but also because it was easy and the kids were cute.

Today, a new volunteer was there. Her name was Kiera, and she was... different.

Kiera had vitiligo, patches of lighter skin scattered across her dark arms and face like a map of continents. She wore her hair in natural coils, no makeup, and a bright yellow dress that made her look like sunshine.

Rachel couldn't stop staring, then felt immediately guilty about it.

"Hi! You must be Rachel," Kiera said, walking over with a huge smile. "Mrs. Johnson said you'd show me the ropes."

"Yeah, um, hi." Rachel tucked her hair behind her ear self-consciously. "It's pretty easy. We just set up activities and make sure the kids don't destroy anything."

Kiera laughed, a genuine, unselfconscious sound that filled the whole room. "Sounds perfect. I love working with kids."

Over the next few days, Rachel noticed something strange about Kiera. She was... happy. Like, genuinely, effortlessly happy. She didn't check her reflection every five minutes. She didn't adjust her clothes or worry about angles when someone took photos. She just existed, comfortably, in her own skin.

It was confusing. And kind of annoying.

One afternoon, a little girl named Maya was crying because some boys had called her "ugly" for having braces and glasses.

Rachel handed her a tissue. "Don't listen to them, Maya. They're just being mean."

But Kiera knelt down to Maya's level, taking her small hands. "You know what I think? I think those boys don't understand what beauty really is."

"What do you mean?" Maya sniffled.

"Well, tell me something. What's your favorite thing to do?"

"I like to draw," Maya said quietly.

"And when you're drawing, do you feel beautiful?"

Maya looked confused. "I don't think about it."

"Exactly!" Kiera smiled. "Because real beauty isn't about how you look. It's about how you make other people feel. It's about what lights you up inside. When you're drawing, I bet your whole face changes. Your eyes get excited. Your smile gets bigger. That's beauty. That's the real thing."

Maya thought about this, her tears slowing. "But everyone says pretty girls have to look a certain way."

"Everyone is wrong sometimes," Kiera said gently. "Look at me. See these patches on my skin? When I was your age, I hated them. I thought they made me ugly. But you know what I learned? They make me unique. They're part of my story. And my story is beautiful, even if it doesn't look like everyone else's."

Maya touched one of Kiera's patches gently. "I think they're pretty. Like a pattern."

"Thank you, sweetheart. And I think your braces are pretty too. They're helping your teeth grow strong. That's something to be proud of, not ashamed of."

After Maya ran off to join the other kids, Rachel stood there, something tight in her chest.

That evening, Rachel found Kiera sitting outside on the steps, journaling.

"Hey," Rachel said, sitting down next to her. "That thing you said to Maya earlier. About beauty. Did you really mean it?"

Kiera looked up, closing her journal. "Every word. Why?"

"I just..." Rachel picked at her nail polish. "I don't know. It's easy to say that stuff to a kid. But in the real world, people do judge you by how you look. Like, constantly."

"They do," Kiera agreed. "But that says more about them than it does about you."

"But don't you ever feel... I don't know... ugly? Because of your skin?"

Kiera was quiet for a moment. "I used to. When I was younger, I tried everything to hide it. Makeup, long sleeves, staying out of the sun. I spent so much energy trying to look 'normal' that I forgot to actually live."

"What changed?"

"My grandma died," Kiera said softly. "She was the most beautiful person I ever knew. Not because of how she looked, but because of how she loved. How she laughed. How she made everyone around her feel seen and valued. At her funeral, nobody talked about her appearance. They talked about her kindness, her strength, her joy. And I realized, that's what I want people to remember about me too. Not whether my skin matched society's standards, but whether I made the world a little brighter."

Rachel felt tears prick her eyes. "I spend like two hours getting ready every morning. And I still feel ugly."

"That's because you're looking for beauty in the wrong place," Kiera said gently. "You're looking in the mirror. But beauty isn't a reflection. It's a radiation. It comes from inside."

"That sounds like something from a poster in a guidance counselor's office."

Kiera laughed. "It does, doesn't it? But it's true anyway. Rachel, I've watched you with these kids this week. The way you're patient with them. The way you remember all their names and their favorite colors. The way you helped that little boy with his art project even though he got paint all over your shirt. That's beautiful. That's the stuff that actually matters."

The next morning, Rachel stood in front of her bathroom mirror again. But this time, instead of cataloging her flaws, she tried to see herself the way Kiera might see her. The way the kids at the center saw her.

She saw someone who showed up. Someone who cared. Someone who was trying, even when it was hard.

She washed off half her makeup. Then she put on a shirt she actually liked, not just one that made her look thinner. She left her hair natural instead of straightening it.

It felt weird. Vulnerable. But also... lighter, somehow.

At the community center, one of the little girls, Emma, ran up to Rachel immediately.

"Miss Rachel! You look so pretty today!"

Rachel almost laughed. She was wearing less makeup than ever. "Really?"

"Yeah! You look happy. When people are happy, they're always pretty."

Out of the mouths of babes, Rachel thought.

Kiera caught her eye from across the room and smiled, giving her a thumbs up.

That night, Rachel started going through her camera roll, looking at all the selfies she'd taken and deleted over the past year. Hundreds of them. All at different angles, different filters, different desperate attempts to look like someone else's version of beautiful.

She deleted most of them. Then she took one new photo. Just her face, no filter, natural light, a small smile.

She didn't post it. She didn't need to. She just saved it, a reminder that this version of herself, the real one, was worth keeping.

Her sister Nicole knocked on her door. "Hey, I'm ordering pizza. Want some?"

"Yeah, definitely." Rachel set down her phone. "Hey, Nicole?"

"Yeah?"

"Do you think I'm pretty?"

Nicole looked at her for a long moment. "I think you're beautiful when you stop trying so hard to be beautiful. Like right now. When you're just... you."

Rachel smiled. It wasn't the answer she'd been fishing for. It was better.

The last day of the summer program, Kiera gave Rachel a hug goodbye.

"You know what I'm going to remember most about you?" Kiera asked.

"What?"

"The way you light up when you're helping those kids. The way you really listen to them. The way you care, even when you think nobody's watching. That's the beauty I'm going to remember."

Rachel hugged her tighter. "Thank you. For everything."

"Just promise me something," Kiera said, pulling back to look at her. "Promise me you'll stop looking for your worth in mirrors and start finding it in moments. In the things you do, the people you love, the difference you make. That's where real beauty lives."

"I promise," Rachel said. And for the first time in a long time, she actually believed it.

Reflect & Grow

Questions for you:

- *When you think about beauty, what standards are you measuring yourself against? Where did those standards come from?*
- *Think of someone you consider beautiful. Is it really their appearance, or is it something else about them that draws you in?*
- *What are three things you do that make the world more beautiful, that have nothing to do with how you look?*
- *If you spent less time worrying about your appearance, what would you do with that time and energy?*

Remember: You are not ornamental. You are not here to be looked at. You are here to live, to love, to create, to connect. Your beauty is not in your mirror selfie. It's in your laugh, your kindness, your courage, your care. It's in the way you make others feel seen. That's the beauty that lasts. That's the beauty that matters. That's the beauty you already are.

Courage Isn't the Absence of Fear

Mia Rodriguez stared at the sign-up sheet on the bulletin board like it might bite her.

SPRING TALENT SHOW Sign up to perform! All acts welcome!

Her best friend Jamie nudged her shoulder. "Come on, Mia. You have to do it. You're an amazing singer."

"In my bedroom," Mia said quickly. "With the door closed. That's very different from singing in front of the entire school."

"But you love singing! You're always humming, always making up little songs. Why not share that with people?"

Because sharing meant people could judge. People could laugh. People could see her fail.

"I just... I can't," Mia said, turning away from the sign-up sheet. "I'm not brave like you."

Jamie performed in the talent show every year. Dance routines, comedy sketches, once even a magic act that went hilariously wrong. But Jamie never seemed scared. She just did things.

"Mia, I'm terrified every single time," Jamie said. "I just do it anyway."

"That's not the same thing."

"Isn't it?"

That night at dinner, Mia's abuela noticed she was quiet.

"Que pasa, mija? You're pushing your food around like it did something wrong."

Mia sighed. "There's a talent show at school. Jamie thinks I should sign up to sing."

"And what do you think?"

"I think I'd throw up from fear before I even made it on stage."

Her abuela laughed, that warm, knowing laugh that always made Mia feel seen. "Let me tell you a story. When I was your age, back in Mexico, I had to give a speech in front of my entire school. I was so scared, I actually did throw up. Right before going on stage."

"Abuela, that's not helping."

"Wait, I'm not finished. I threw up, I cleaned myself up, and then I went on stage anyway. My legs were shaking so bad I thought I might fall over. My voice cracked twice. But I did it. And you know what I learned?"

"That public speaking is terrible?"

"That courage isn't about not being afraid. It's about being afraid and doing it anyway." Abuela reached across the table and squeezed Mia's hand. "Brave people aren't the ones who feel no fear. They're the ones who feel the fear and still take the step."

Mia thought about that long after dinner was over.

The next day, Mia found herself walking past the sign-up sheet three times. Each time, she told herself she was just going to write her name. Each time, she walked away.

On the fourth pass, she literally bumped into someone. Papers scattered everywhere.

"Oh my gosh, I'm so sorry!" Mia dropped to her knees, helping gather the papers.

"No worries," the girl said. It was Hannah Lee, a senior Mia barely knew. "I wasn't watching where I was going."

Mia handed her the papers and noticed they were sheet music. "Are you signing up for the talent show?"

"Yeah, piano performance. Fourth year in a row." Hannah smiled, but it looked strained.

"You must not get nervous anymore, doing it so many times."

Hannah laughed, but it was sharp. "Are you kidding? I'm having a panic attack just thinking about it. Last night I dreamed I forgot the entire piece and just sat there at the piano in silence while everyone stared at me."

Mia blinked. "But you're signing up anyway?"

"Of course. Being scared isn't a good enough reason not to do something you love." Hannah looked at the empty sign-up sheet in Mia's hand. "You thinking about it?"

"Maybe. I don't know. I'm not brave enough."

"Here's a secret," Hannah said, leaning in like she was sharing classified information. "Nobody is brave enough. We're all just faking it until we make it. The difference between people who perform and people who don't isn't courage. It's just... the willingness to be scared in public instead of scared in private."

She signed her name with a flourish and handed the pen to Mia. "Your turn to be scared in public."

Before Mia could overthink it, Hannah walked away, leaving her alone with the sign-up sheet and a pen that suddenly felt very heavy.

Mia's hand shook as she wrote her name. The moment the pen left the paper, she wanted to erase it, to run, to pretend it never happened.

But it was done.

"Oh my God, you did it!" Jamie appeared out of nowhere, pulling Mia into a hug. "I'm so proud of you!"

"I'm going to regret this," Mia said, but she was smiling despite herself.

"Probably," Jamie agreed cheerfully. "But you'll regret not doing it more."

The next two weeks were torture. Mia practiced every day, her voice shaking through every run-through. She picked a song she loved, a ballad about finding your strength, but every time she sang it, all she could think about was forgetting the words or hitting a wrong note or having her voice crack at the worst possible moment.

The night before the talent show, Mia couldn't sleep. She lay in bed, staring at the ceiling, her heart racing.

Around midnight, there was a soft knock on her door. Her abuela peeked in.

"Can't sleep, mija?"

"I'm thinking about backing out," Mia admitted. "I can still pull my name from the list. I can say I'm sick. Nobody would blame me."

Abuela sat on the edge of the bed. "You could do that. But let me ask you something. What's the worst thing that could happen?"

"I could mess up. I could embarrass myself. Everyone could laugh at me."

"Okay. And then what?"

"What do you mean?"

"I mean, say all those things happen. Say you mess up completely. Then what? Does the school explode? Do you turn into a frog? What actually happens?"

Mia thought about it. "I guess... life goes on."

"Exactly. Life goes on. The sun comes up the next day. You go back to school. Maybe some people remember it, maybe they don't. But you know what you'll remember? You'll remember that you tried. That you were brave enough to step on that stage even though you were terrified. And that, mija, is worth more than a perfect performance."

"But what if I'm not good enough?"

"Good enough for who? The judges? Random kids in the audience who wouldn't have the courage to get up there themselves?" Abuela shook her head. "Mia, you're already good enough. The performance isn't what makes you worthy. You're worthy because you're you. The performance is just you sharing a tiny piece of that with the world."

The night of the talent show, Mia stood backstage, her palms sweating, her heart threatening to beat out of her chest. She could hear the audience beyond the curtain, hundreds of people.

Jamie was doing her dance routine, killing it as always. The audience loved her. Of course they did. Jamie was confident, skilled, fearless.

Mia was none of those things.

"Mia Rodriguez, you're up next," the stage manager said.

This was it. She could still back out. She could still...

But then she thought about her abuela. About Hannah. About Jamie saying she was terrified every time but did it anyway.

Courage isn't the absence of fear. It's feeling the fear and taking the step.

Mia took the step.

The stage lights were blinding. She couldn't see individual faces in the audience, which was somehow both terrifying and comforting. She gripped the microphone, and for one horrible moment, her mind went completely blank.

Then the music started. And somewhere deep inside, muscle memory took over.

She sang.

Her voice shook on the first line. Her hand trembled on the microphone. But she kept going. Line after line, note after note, she pushed through the fear.

And somewhere around the second verse, something shifted. She stopped thinking about the audience. She stopped thinking about messing up. She just... sang. Because she loved it. Because the song meant something to her. Because this was her moment, imperfect and terrifying and absolutely hers.

When the last note faded, there was a split second of silence. Mia's heart dropped. They hated it. They...

Then the applause started. Not polite, scattered clapping, but real, genuine applause. Some people were even standing.

Mia barely remembered walking off stage. Jamie grabbed her in a crushing hug. "You were amazing! Your voice was incredible!"

"I was shaking the whole time," Mia said.

"I know! I could see it from the audience. But you did it anyway. That's the most badass thing ever."

Later that night, Mia sat with her abuela in the kitchen, drinking hot chocolate like they always did after big events.

"So," Abuela said, "how do you feel?"

Mia thought about it. "Proud. Scared. Relieved. All at the same time."

"That sounds about right." Abuela smiled. "You know what you did tonight, mija? You showed yourself what you're capable of. Not because you weren't afraid, but because you were afraid and you did it anyway. That's the real lesson. Fear doesn't have to stop you. It can just... come along for the ride."

"I don't think I'll ever not be scared of performing."

"Good. If you're not scared, it probably doesn't matter enough to you." Abuela touched Mia's cheek gently. "Brave people aren't the ones without fear. They're the ones whose love is bigger than their fear. And tonight, your love of music was bigger than your fear of judgment. That's courage."

Mia thought about next year's talent show. The thought still made her nervous. But now she knew something she didn't know before.

She could do scary things. She could feel the fear and do it anyway. She could be brave, not because she wasn't afraid, but because she was.

And that changed everything.

Reflect & Grow

Questions for you:

- *What's something you've wanted to do but fear has held you back from trying?*
- *Can you remember a time you did something scary? How did you feel afterward? Was it worth it?*
- *What's the difference between being reckless and being courageous? How do you know when fear is protecting you vs when it's limiting you?*
- *If fear wasn't a factor, what would you try tomorrow?*

Remember: Courage isn't about being fearless. It's about deciding that what you want is more important than what you're afraid of. Every brave person you've ever admired has been scared. They just didn't let that fear make the decision for them. Your fear is valid, but it doesn't have to be in charge. You can acknowledge it, thank it for trying to protect you, and then do the thing anyway. That's not just courage. That's growth.

Failure Is Your Best Teacher

J ordan Mitchell had never failed at anything important in her life. Until today.

She stared at the list posted outside the gym, scanning it three times, four times, hoping her eyes were playing tricks on her. But no matter how many times she looked, her name wasn't there.

She hadn't made the varsity basketball team.

"Jordan?" Her teammate Aisha touched her shoulder gently. "I'm so sorry."

Jordan couldn't speak. Basketball was her thing. She'd been playing since she was six. She'd been on every team, won every local championship, been named MVP twice. Basketball wasn't just what she did. It was who she was.

And now, apparently, she wasn't good enough.

"At least you made JV," Aisha offered. "That's still..."

"JV is for freshmen," Jordan said, her voice flat. "I'm a junior. This is humiliating."

She walked away before Aisha could say anything else, before anyone could see the tears building behind her eyes.

At home, Jordan went straight to her room and slammed the door. She looked at the wall covered in basketball photos and trophies. Championship medals. Newspaper clippings. A signed jersey from her favorite WNBA player.

All of it felt like a lie now.

Her mom knocked softly. "Jordan? Aisha's mom called. She told me what happened. Can I come in?"

"I don't want to talk about it."

Her mom came in anyway, sitting on the edge of the bed. "Honey, I know you're disappointed..."

"Disappointed?" Jordan laughed bitterly. "Mom, I've dedicated my entire life to basketball. I wake up at 5 AM to practice. I watch game films on weekends. I gave up hanging out with friends to train. And it wasn't enough. I wasn't enough."

"That's not what this means."

"Then what does it mean? That I'm not as good as I thought I was? That all those hours were wasted?"

Her mom was quiet for a moment. "Can I tell you about the time I didn't get into medical school?"

Jordan looked up, surprised. Her mom was a successful doctor. She'd never mentioned failing.

"I applied to ten schools my senior year of college. I was sure I'd get in somewhere. I had good grades, good test scores, good recommendations. I got rejected from all ten."

"What did you do?"

"I cried for a week. Then I worked as a medical assistant for a year, retook some classes, volunteered at a clinic, and reapplied. I got into three schools the second time around. And you know what? That year of 'failure' made me a better doctor. It taught me humility. It taught me that setbacks aren't endings, they're redirections."

"This feels like an ending," Jordan said quietly.

"I know it does. But it's not. It's just a really hard middle."

The first JV practice was brutal. Not because the drills were hard, but because Jordan's ego kept getting in the way. She was surrounded by freshmen and sophomores, kids who looked at her with confusion.

"Aren't you Jordan Mitchell?" one freshman asked. "I saw you play last year. You were amazing. Why aren't you on varsity?"

"Because I'm not good enough, apparently," Jordan snapped.

The girl flinched and walked away.

Coach Davis blew his whistle. "Mitchell, in my office. Now."

Jordan followed him, her stomach sinking.

"Listen," Coach Davis said, leaning against his desk. "I know you're angry. I know this feels unfair. But you need to make a choice right now. You can spend this season being bitter and resentful, or you can use it to grow."

"How is playing JV supposed to help me grow? I should be playing at a higher level."

"Should you?" Coach Davis raised an eyebrow. "Jordan, you're talented. Very talented. But do you know why you didn't make varsity?"

Jordan shook her head, not trusting herself to speak.

"Because you play like you're the only person on the court. You don't pass when you should. You take impossible shots instead of setting up your teammates. You've got individual skill, but basketball is a team sport. And until you learn that, all the talent in the world won't matter."

The words hit Jordan like a physical blow. "But I..."

"I'm not saying this to be cruel. I'm saying this because I believe you can be incredible. But first, you need to fail. You need to learn what it feels like to not be the star. To be part of something bigger than yourself. This season isn't a punishment. It's an opportunity. The question is, are you going to take it?"

Jordan spent that night watching old game footage of herself. Really watching, not just admiring her own highlights. And slowly, she started to see what Coach Davis meant.

There. A moment where she could have passed to an open teammate but took a contested shot instead.

There. Another play where she dribbled through three defenders when a simple pass would have led to an easy basket.

There. And there. And there.

She'd been so focused on being the hero that she'd forgotten basketball was a team sport.

The realization was embarrassing. And painful. And necessary.

The next practice, Jordan approached the freshman she'd snapped at.

"Hey, I'm sorry about yesterday. I was taking my frustration out on you, and that wasn't fair."

The girl, whose name turned out to be Maya, smiled tentatively. "It's okay. I can't imagine how hard this must be for you."

"It is hard," Jordan admitted. "But that's not your fault. Fresh start?"

"Fresh start," Maya agreed.

During drills, Jordan started paying attention to her teammates. Really paying attention. Maya was fast but struggled with her left hand. Another girl, Brittany, had an incredible shot but was too timid to take it. A third, Sam, was a natural playmaker but kept apologizing every time she made a mistake.

Jordan started adjusting her game. Setting up Maya for drives on her strong side. Feeding Brittany the ball and encouraging her to shoot. Telling Sam to trust her instincts.

"Nice pass, Jordan!" Coach Davis called after Jordan set up Brittany for a perfect three-pointer.

It was the first compliment Jordan had received all week, and it felt different than the praise she was used to. Better, somehow. Like she'd earned it in a new way.

Three weeks into the season, JV played their first game. Jordan started on the bench.

It stung. Star players didn't sit on the bench. But she'd promised herself she'd use this season to grow, not to sulk.

When Coach finally put her in during the second quarter, Jordan played differently than she ever had before. She passed first, shot second. She called out plays. She celebrated her teammates' baskets as loudly as her own.

And something magical happened. The team clicked. They moved like a unit, trusting each other, supporting each other. They won by fifteen points.

In the locker room after, Maya high-fived her. "That was incredible! The way you set up Sam for that final basket was perfect."

"We all did it," Jordan said. And she meant it.

Halfway through the season, something unexpected happened. The varsity team was struggling. They had talent, but they weren't playing together. They were losing games they should have won.

Jordan went to watch one of their games, sitting in the stands with her JV teammates. It was strange, watching from the outside. But also educational.

"They're not passing," Sam observed.

"Everyone's trying to be the star," Brittany added.

Jordan nodded slowly. That could have been her. That would have been her.

After the game, Coach Thompson, the varsity coach, approached Jordan in the parking lot.

"You've been playing well on JV," she said.

"Thank you, Coach."

"I made a mistake at tryouts. I was looking for individual talent, and I missed something important. You're a better player now than you were then. If you're interested, I'd like you to practice with varsity, see how it goes."

Jordan's heart leaped. This was what she'd wanted. What she'd been working toward.

But then she thought about her JV team. About Maya and Brittany and Sam. About the progress they'd all made together.

"Can I think about it?" Jordan asked.

Coach Thompson looked surprised but nodded. "Sure. Let me know by Monday."

That weekend, Jordan talked to Coach Davis.

"What should I do?" she asked.

"What do you want to do?"

"I want to play at the highest level I can. But I also... I don't want to abandon my team. We've built something special."

Coach Davis smiled. "Jordan, do you know what I've been most impressed by this season? Not your scoring or your athleticism. It's your growth. You came here angry and humbled, and you could have stayed bitter. Instead, you became a leader. You made everyone around you better. That's the mark of a truly great player."

"So you think I should go to varsity?"

"I think you should do what's best for your growth. But remember, being the best player in the room isn't always where you learn the most. Sometimes the best growth happens in the struggle."

Monday morning, Jordan told Coach Thompson her decision.

"I appreciate the offer, Coach. Really. But I want to finish the season with JV. We've got something special building, and I don't want to walk away from that. Plus, I'm still learning. I'm not ready yet."

Coach Thompson studied her for a long moment. "You know what? You're more ready than you think. But I respect your decision. Finish strong with your team. There's always next year."

As Jordan walked away, she felt lighter than she had in months. She'd chosen her team over her ego. She'd chosen growth over glory.

And somehow, that felt like the biggest win of all.

At the end of the season, JV won their division championship. In the final game, Jordan had eight assists and only twelve points. It was her lowest scoring game of the season.

It was also her best.

When Coach Davis handed her the trophy, he said, "You know what failure taught you this year?"

"What?"

"That success isn't about being the best. It's about bringing out the best in everyone around you. You failed your way into becoming a real leader. That's worth more than any varsity spot."

Jordan looked at her teammates, at the trophy, at the journey that had brought them here. Her mom had been right. This wasn't an ending. It was a beginning.

And the failure that had felt like the end of the world? It turned out to be the best teacher she'd ever had.

Reflect & Grow

Questions for you:

- Think of a time you failed at something important. What did that experience teach you?

- What's the difference between failing and being a failure? How can you separate your worth from your outcomes?

- Are there areas in your life where you're afraid to try because you might fail? What would you attempt if failure wasn't so scary?

- Who in your life has failed and grown from it? What can you learn from their experience?

Remember: Failure isn't the opposite of success. It's part of the path to success. Every person you admire has failed, probably multiple times. The difference is they didn't let failure define them. They let it teach them. Your failures are not reflections of your worth. They're feedback, showing you where to grow, what to change, how to improve. Embrace them. Learn from them. And then get back up and try again, wiser than before.

Your Comfort Zone Is Where Dreams Go to Die

Every day was exactly the same for Charlotte Hayes. Wake up at 6:30. Shower. Same breakfast. Same route to school. Same friends at lunch. Same classes. Same homework routine. Same TV shows at night. Same bedtime.

It was comfortable. Predictable. Safe.

It was also slowly suffocating her.

Charlotte sat in the library during study hall, doodling in the margins of her notebook instead of doing homework. She drew the same thing she always drew: faraway places. Mountains she'd never climbed. Cities she'd never visited. Adventures she'd never have.

"Those are really good," a voice said.

Charlotte looked up to see Jade Chen, a girl from her English class who always seemed to be doing something interesting. Last month it was rock climbing. This month she'd started a podcast. Jade was the kind of person who tried everything.

"Thanks," Charlotte said, quickly closing her notebook. "They're just doodles."

"They don't look like just doodles. They look like dreams." Jade sat down across from her. "Have you ever been to any of those places?"

"No. I've barely been outside of Ohio."

"So why don't you go?"

Charlotte laughed. "Because I'm seventeen and broke and have school and responsibilities?"

"I'm not saying hop on a plane to Paris tomorrow. But like, why don't you do something? Anything different?" Jade pulled out a flyer from her bag. "There's this outdoor adventure club that does weekend trips. Hiking, camping, kayaking. It's super cheap because the school sponsors it. You should come."

Charlotte looked at the flyer. A weekend camping trip in the state forest. It sounded terrifying. Sleeping outside? With bugs? With people she didn't know?

"I don't know. That's not really my thing."

"What is your thing?" Jade asked, not unkindly.

Charlotte opened her mouth to answer and realized she didn't have one. Her "thing" was... being comfortable. Being safe. Being exactly where she'd always been.

"That's what I thought," Jade said gently. "Look, I'm not trying to pressure you. But that look on your face when you draw those places? That's not the look of someone who's happy with comfortable. That's the look of someone who's dreaming of more."

That night, Charlotte stared at the flyer on her desk. The trip was in two weeks. All she had to do was sign up.

But the thought of it made her stomach twist. What if she hated camping? What if she couldn't keep up on the hikes? What if everyone else knew what they were doing and she looked stupid?

Her older brother, Tyler, poked his head in her room. "Hey, Mom wants to know if you want the usual for dinner."

"The usual" was Friday night pizza. The same order they'd been getting for ten years.

"Actually," Charlotte heard herself say, "can we try that new Thai place instead?"

Tyler raised his eyebrows. "You? Miss Creature-of-Habit wants to try something new? Are you feeling okay?"

"I'm fine. I just... I want to try something different."

At dinner, Charlotte ordered something she couldn't pronounce and had no idea what it would taste like. When it arrived, it was spicy and strange and nothing like what she usually ate.

It was also delicious.

"Look at you, being adventurous," her mom said, smiling. "What brought this on?"

Charlotte thought about the flyer in her room. About Jade's question. About the drawings in her notebook that were always of somewhere else.

"I think I've been playing it too safe," Charlotte admitted. "I think I've been so comfortable that I forgot there's a whole world out there."

Her dad looked thoughtful. "You know, when I was your age, I was a lot like you. I liked routines, liked knowing what to expect. Then my best friend convinced me to take a road trip the summer after graduation. Completely spontaneous. We didn't even have a plan."

"What happened?"

"Best summer of my life. We got lost, we ran out of money, we slept in the car, and it was incredible. It taught me that the magic happens outside your comfort zone." He smiled. "I'm not saying you should drop everything and hitchhike across the country. But maybe... try one thing that scares you. See what happens."

Charlotte signed up for the camping trip.

The two weeks leading up to it were torture. She almost backed out five times. But every time she thought about staying home, she thought about her dad's story. She thought about her drawings. She thought about Jade's question: what is your thing?

The morning of the trip, Charlotte's hands shook as she packed her borrowed sleeping bag and tent. She'd never camped before. She didn't know what she was doing.

But she showed up anyway.

The group was small, about fifteen students and two adult leaders. Jade waved enthusiastically when she saw Charlotte.

"You came! I'm so glad!"

"I'm terrified," Charlotte admitted.

"Good. That means you're doing something worth doing."

The drive to the forest took two hours. Charlotte spent most of it silent, listening to the others chat excitedly about previous trips and what they hoped to see. These people all seemed so comfortable with adventure. So confident.

Charlotte felt like an imposter.

Setting up camp was harder than it looked. Charlotte struggled with her tent for twenty minutes before a guy named Marcus came over to help.

"First time camping?" he asked, not judgmentally, just curious.

"Is it that obvious?"

"Only because I was the same way on my first trip. Couldn't figure out the tent poles to save my life." He showed her the trick to it. "The first time doing anything is always the hardest. But that's also when you grow the most."

Once camp was set up, the group went on a hike. Charlotte, who never exercised beyond gym class, struggled to keep up. Her lungs burned. Her legs ached. She wanted to quit.

But then they reached the top of the ridge, and Charlotte saw the view.

Miles and miles of forest, stretching out like a green ocean. The sky impossibly blue. Mountains in the distance. It was like stepping into one of her drawings.

"Worth it?" Jade asked, appearing beside her.

Charlotte couldn't speak. She just nodded, tears prickling her eyes. Not from sadness, but from something else. Relief, maybe. Or recognition. Like she'd been looking for this feeling her whole life without knowing it.

That night around the campfire, people shared stories. Adventures they'd had, places they wanted to go, things they wanted to try. Charlotte mostly listened, but at some point, someone passed her a marshmallow stick.

"What about you, Charlotte? What's something you've always wanted to do?"

Everyone looked at her. A month ago, Charlotte would have said "nothing" and changed the subject. But something had shifted in her on that ridge.

"I want to travel," she said quietly. Then louder, "I want to see the places I draw. I want to hike mountains and visit cities and try food I can't pronounce. I want to stop being so afraid of everything."

"So what's stopping you?" Marcus asked.

"Fear, I guess. Fear of the unknown. Fear of failing. Fear of being uncomfortable."

"But you're here," Jade pointed out. "Camping in the woods when you've never done it before. You're already doing the scary thing."

Charlotte looked around at the dark forest, the crackling fire, the faces of near-strangers who felt like friends. "Yeah. I guess I am."

"How does it feel?" someone asked.

Charlotte thought about it. "Terrifying. But also... alive. I feel more alive than I have in years."

The next morning, Charlotte woke up sore and tired and covered in mosquito bites. She'd barely slept on the hard ground. She was cold and achy and desperately wanted a hot shower.

She'd also never been happier.

They spent the day kayaking on a nearby lake. Charlotte had never been in a kayak before and spent the first ten minutes going in circles. But eventually she got the hang of it, paddling out to the middle of the lake where the water was glass-smooth and the world was quiet.

"This is what I've been missing," Charlotte said to Jade, who'd paddled up beside her. "I've been so focused on staying safe that I forgot to actually live."

"The comfort zone is a beautiful place," Jade said, "but nothing ever grows there."

Charlotte thought about her life back home. Her routine. Her same breakfast, same friends, same everything. It had felt safe. But had it felt alive?

No. It had felt like sleepwalking.

On the drive home, Charlotte's mind was racing. Not with anxiety this time, but with possibilities. What else could she try? What other adventures were waiting outside her comfort zone?

That week, Charlotte signed up for three things she'd never done before: a pottery class, a hiking club, and an SAT prep course at a different school where she didn't know anyone.

Were they all scary? Yes. Did she want to back out of every single one? Absolutely.

But she didn't. She showed up. She tried. She stumbled and made mistakes and felt awkward.

She also met new people, learned new skills, and discovered parts of herself she didn't know existed.

In pottery class, she was terrible at first. Her bowls collapsed, her vases were lopsided. But the teacher, an older woman with clay-stained fingers, just smiled.

"You're learning. That's the point. Too many people quit before they get to the good part because they can't handle being bad at something first."

Charlotte looked at her collapsed bowl. Then she rolled up her sleeves and started again.

Two months later, Charlotte stood in front of her English class, giving a presentation she'd volunteered for. The old Charlotte would never have volunteered. The old Charlotte avoided attention at all costs.

But the new Charlotte, the one who'd learned to be uncomfortable, raised her hand.

Her topic was "The Value of Trying New Things." She talked about the camping trip, about being terrified but going anyway. About how growth only happens when you're willing to be bad at something before you get good at it.

"The comfort zone feels safe," Charlotte said, looking out at her classmates. "But it's actually the most dangerous place to stay. Because while you're being comfortable, life is passing you by. Your dreams are waiting for you outside that zone. But you have to be brave enough to step out and meet them."

After class, three different people approached her asking about the outdoor adventure club. One girl said, "I've been wanting to try something new but I've been too scared. You inspired me."

Charlotte thought about the girl she'd been just a few months ago. The one who'd been too scared to try Thai food. And she smiled.

That weekend, Charlotte sat at her desk with her notebook open. But instead of drawing faraway places, she was planning them. Real trips. Real adventures. Some big, some small, but all outside her comfort zone.

Her mom knocked on the door. "Hey, sweetie. Dad and I were talking. We've been doing the same beach vacation every summer for ten years. We thought maybe this year we could go somewhere different. Somewhere you've always wanted to see."

Charlotte looked at her drawings, at her plans, at the person she was becoming.

"I'd like that," she said. "I'd like that a lot."

Because she'd learned something important over the past few months. The comfort zone wasn't actually comfortable. It was just familiar. And familiar wasn't the same as fulfilling.

Dreams didn't live in the safe spaces. They lived in the scary ones, the uncertain ones, the ones that made your heart race and your hands shake.

And Charlotte was done watching her dreams from a distance. She was ready to chase them.

One uncomfortable, terrifying, wonderful step at a time.

Reflect & Grow

Questions for you:

- What does your "comfort zone" look like? What routines or habits do you cling to because they're familiar, even if they're not fulfilling?
- What's something you've always wanted to try but fear has kept you from attempting?

- Think of a time you stepped outside your comfort zone. How did it feel? What did you learn?
- If you knew you couldn't fail, what would you try tomorrow?

Remember: Your comfort zone will always be there, waiting for you if you need it. But so will your dreams, your growth, and your potential. The magic, the adventure, the person you're meant to become, they're all waiting just outside that comfortable bubble. Yes, it's scary out there. Yes, you might fail. Yes, you'll be uncomfortable. But you'll also be alive in a way you've never been before. And that's worth every uncomfortable moment.

Vulnerability Is Real Strength

A lex Carter never cried. Not at sad movies, not at funerals, not even when she broke her arm in sixth grade.

Crying was weakness. Asking for help was weakness. Showing emotion was weakness.

At least, that's what Alex had always believed.

She sat alone in the school bathroom during lunch, scrolling through her phone, pretending everything was fine. Her grades were slipping. Her parents were fighting constantly. Her best friend had moved across the country over the summer. And last week, her dog of twelve years had died.

But Alex was fine. Totally fine. She didn't need to talk about it. She didn't need help. She could handle it.

A text from her mom popped up: *Dad and I need to talk to you tonight. It's important.*

Alex's stomach dropped. She knew what that meant. She'd seen this coming for months. But knowing didn't make it hurt any less.

She deleted the message and went to class like nothing was wrong. Because that's what strong people did. They didn't fall apart. They held it together.

In English class, Mrs. Palmer assigned partners for a project on poetry. Alex got paired with Riley Santos, a quiet girl who always sat in the front row and actually seemed to care about literature.

"Hey," Riley said, sliding into the desk next to Alex. "Want to meet at the library after school to work on this?"

"Sure. Whatever."

Riley looked at her for a moment, her expression thoughtful. "Are you okay?"

"I'm fine," Alex said automatically. "Why wouldn't I be?"

"You just seem... I don't know. Distant lately."

"I'm fine," Alex repeated, more firmly this time. "Let's just focus on the project."

Riley nodded but didn't look convinced.

At the library that afternoon, they worked in silence for a while. The assignment was to choose a poem and write about what it revealed about human vulnerability.

"What does vulnerability even mean?" Alex muttered, staring at the page. "Like, being weak?"

"I don't think so," Riley said. "I think it means being honest about how you feel, even when it's hard."

"Same thing."

"Is it though?" Riley set down her pen. "I used to think that too. That showing emotion made you weak. That asking for help meant you couldn't handle things on your own."

"And now?"

"Now I think pretending to be okay when you're not is actually way harder than just being honest." Riley paused. "My parents got divorced last year. And I spent months acting like it didn't affect me. Like I was totally fine with moving between two houses and having split holidays and watching my family fall apart."

Alex looked up, surprised. Riley always seemed so put together, so calm.

"But I wasn't fine," Riley continued. "I was drowning. And the thing that saved me wasn't being strong enough to handle it alone. It was being brave enough to admit I couldn't."

Alex felt something crack inside her chest. "What did you do?"

"I told my school counselor I was struggling. I started seeing a therapist. I talked to my parents about how I was really feeling instead of just saying I was fine." Riley smiled sadly. "It was the hardest thing I've ever done. Way harder than pretending everything was okay. But it was also the thing that actually helped."

That night, Alex sat at the dinner table with her parents, waiting for the conversation she'd been dreading.

"Alex, honey," her mom started, reaching across the table. "Your dad and I have been talking, and we've decided..."

"You're getting divorced," Alex said flatly. "I know. It's fine."

Her parents exchanged a look.

"Sweetie, it's not fine," her dad said gently. "This is a big change for all of us. It's okay to be upset about it."

"But I'm not upset. I saw this coming. It's whatever."

"Alex," her mom said softly, "you don't have to be strong about this. You're allowed to have feelings."

"I do have feelings. I feel fine." Alex stood up. "Can I be excused? I have homework."

She went to her room before they could see the tears she refused to let fall.

Over the next week, Alex doubled down on being "fine." She smiled at school. She laughed at jokes. She pretended like nothing was wrong, even as her world was crumbling.

But her body was keeping score. She couldn't sleep. She couldn't focus. She snapped at people for no reason. Her chest felt tight all the time, like she couldn't quite catch her breath.

In the library, working on the poetry project, Riley noticed.

"Alex, your hands are shaking."

Alex looked down. She hadn't even realized. "I'm just tired."

"Alex." Riley's voice was gentle but firm. "You're not fine. And that's okay. You don't have to be fine."

"Yes, I do," Alex said, her voice cracking. "If I'm not fine, if I fall apart, then everything falls apart. I have to hold it together."

"For who?"

The question stopped Alex cold. "What?"

"Who are you holding it together for? Your parents? They already know they're getting divorced. Your friends? They probably already know something's wrong. So who?"

Alex opened her mouth to answer and realized she didn't have one. She'd been holding it together for... herself? For some idea of who she thought she should be?

"I just..." Alex felt the words catch in her throat. "I just don't want to be weak."

"Asking for help isn't weak," Riley said. "Pretending you don't need it is. Do you know how much strength it takes to admit you're struggling? To be vulnerable with people? That's not weakness, Alex. That's the bravest thing you can do."

And suddenly, all the feelings Alex had been shoving down for weeks, months, maybe years, came flooding up. The tears she'd been holding back broke free. Her shoulders shook. Her breath came in gasps.

She was crying in the school library, and she couldn't stop, and it was terrifying and humiliating and...

Liberating.

Riley didn't tell her to stop or calm down or pull herself together. She just sat there, a quiet presence, letting Alex fall apart without judgment.

When the tears finally slowed, Alex felt exhausted. But also lighter, like she'd been carrying something heavy and had finally set it down.

"I'm sorry," Alex said, wiping her face. "That was..."

"Human," Riley finished. "That was human. And there's nothing to apologize for."

That night, Alex did something she'd never done before. She knocked on her parents' bedroom door and said, "Can we talk? Actually talk?"

They sat in the living room, and for the first time, Alex didn't pretend to be fine.

"I'm really sad about the divorce," she said, her voice shaking. "And I'm scared about what it means. And I'm angry that our family is changing. And I miss Buddy." Her voice broke on her dog's name. "I miss him so much and I never let myself grieve because I thought I had to be strong."

Her mom pulled her into a hug, and this time, Alex let herself lean in.

"You are strong," her dad said, his own eyes wet. "But strength doesn't mean not feeling things. It means feeling them and not letting them destroy you."

"I don't know how to do that," Alex admitted.

"We'll figure it out together," her mom said. "Maybe we could all see a family therapist? Work through this as a team?"

Alex nodded, still crying, but feeling more solid than she had in months.

The next day at school, Alex approached the guidance counselor's office. She stood outside for five minutes, her hand on the doorknob, every instinct screaming at her to turn around.

But she thought about Riley's words. About real strength. About vulnerability.

She opened the door.

"Hi," she said to Ms. Washington, the counselor. "I'm Alex Carter. I need help. I'm not okay, and I don't know how to fix it on my own."

Ms. Washington smiled warmly. "Thank you for coming in, Alex. It takes a lot of courage to ask for help. Let's talk."

Over the next few weeks, Alex learned what vulnerability actually meant. It meant telling her English teacher she was struggling to keep up because of stress at home. It meant accepting extensions on assignments instead of pretending she could handle everything. It meant being honest with her friends about why she'd been distant.

It meant letting people see her, really see her, even the messy, struggling parts.

And the strangest thing happened. People didn't think less of her. They respected her more. Teachers offered support. Friends reached out. People shared their own struggles, creating connections Alex had never experienced when she was busy pretending to be invulnerable.

In the library one afternoon, Riley smiled at her. "You seem different. Better."

"I feel different," Alex admitted. "Lighter. Like I've been carrying around this armor that was actually just making everything harder."

"Armor's heavy," Riley said. "Vulnerability is lighter. Scarier, but lighter."

"I always thought being vulnerable meant being weak. But it's actually the opposite. It takes so much more strength to admit you need help than to pretend you don't."

"Now you sound like a motivational poster," Riley teased.

Alex laughed. "I know. But it's true anyway."

For their poetry project, Alex chose a poem by Naomi Shihab Nye called "Kindness." There was a line in it that struck her: "Before you know kindness as the deepest thing inside, you must know sorrow as the other deepest thing."

In her essay, Alex wrote about how she'd spent so long trying to avoid sorrow, trying to armor herself against pain, that she'd also armored herself against connection, against help, against kindness.

"Vulnerability isn't about being broken," she wrote. "It's about being brave enough to be honest. To say 'I'm struggling' instead of 'I'm fine.' To ask for help instead of drowning alone. To let people see you, really see you, even when it's scary. That's not weakness. That's the strongest thing a person can do."

Mrs. Palmer wrote at the top of her essay: "Beautiful and brave. Thank you for sharing this."

Months later, Alex sat with her mom in the family therapist's office. They were talking about the divorce, about feelings, about fears. It was hard. Some sessions, Alex cried. Some sessions, she got angry.

But she wasn't pretending anymore. She wasn't carrying everything alone.

After one particularly difficult session, her mom said, "I'm proud of you, you know. For doing this work. For being so brave."

"I'm not brave," Alex said. "I'm just... tired of pretending."

"That's what bravery is," her mom said. "It's not about being fearless. It's about being real, even when real is terrifying."

Alex thought about the girl she'd been, the one who never cried, who never asked for help, who thought strength meant handling everything alone.

That girl had been drowning.

This girl, the one who cried, who asked for help, who admitted when she was struggling? This girl was learning to swim.

And that made all the difference.

Reflect & Grow

Questions for you:

- When was the last time you pretended to be fine when you weren't? Why did you feel the need to hide your true feelings?

- What does "being strong" mean to you? Does your definition include being honest about when you're struggling?

- Who in your life can you be vulnerable with? Who has earned that trust?

- What would it feel like to ask for help with something you're struggling with? What's holding you back?

Remember: Vulnerability is not weakness. It's the most accurate measure of courage. It takes real strength to admit you don't have all the answers, to ask for help, to let people see you when you're not at your best. The armor you wear to protect yourself from pain also keeps out connection, help, and love. Real strength isn't pretending you're unbreakable. It's being brave enough to show people where you're cracked and trusting they'll help you heal instead of hurt you more.

Change Is the Only Constant

Samantha Brooks hated change. She'd lived in the same house her entire life. Gone to the same school since kindergarten. Had the same best friend since second grade. Her world was stable, predictable, and exactly how she liked it.

Until her mom got the job offer.

"Boston?" Sam stared at her parents across the dinner table. "You want us to move to Boston? That's like a thousand miles away!"

"It's actually about 800 miles," her dad said, trying to lighten the mood. It didn't work.

"This is an incredible opportunity for your mother," he continued. "And for all of us. A fresh start, new experiences..."

"I don't want new experiences!" Sam's voice cracked. "I want my life. My friends. My school. Everything I know is here!"

Her mom reached across the table. "Sweetie, I know this is scary. But sometimes change, even when it's hard, leads to amazing things."

"Or it ruins everything," Sam shot back. "When do we have to decide?"

Her parents exchanged a look. "We already decided," her mom said gently. "We move in six weeks."

Sam felt like the floor had dropped out from under her.

The next day at school, Sam told her best friend Lily about the move. They'd been inseparable since they'd bonded over shared snacks in second grade.

"Six weeks?" Lily's eyes filled with tears. "That's nothing! That's like, tomorrow!"

"I know." Sam felt numb. "I tried to convince them to let me finish the school year here. Maybe stay with my aunt. But they said no."

They sat in silence for a moment, the weight of the change pressing down on both of them.

"What if we lose touch?" Lily asked quietly. "What if you make new friends and forget about me?"

"That's not going to happen," Sam said firmly. "Nothing's going to change between us. Distance doesn't matter."

But even as she said it, Sam wondered if it was true. Everything was changing. How could their friendship stay the same?

Over the next few weeks, Sam tried to hold onto everything as tightly as possible. She took pictures of her room, her street, her favorite spots around town. She made Lily promise to text every day, to video chat every week, to never let their friendship fade.

"I'm trying to freeze time," Sam told her dad one evening as she photographed her bedroom. "If I can capture everything exactly as it is, maybe it won't feel so gone."

Her dad sat on the edge of her bed. "Sam, I know you're scared. Change is scary. But you can't freeze time. Life is constantly moving forward."

"I don't want it to move forward. I like it here."

"I know you do. But think about it. You've changed schools before. From elementary to middle school, from middle school to high school. Those were scary transitions too. But you adapted."

"That was different. I was still in the same town. My friends were still there."

"Some of them," her dad said. "But I bet you have friends now you didn't have in elementary school. People you can't imagine your life without."

Sam thought about it. He was right. Her friend group had shifted over the years. Some friendships had faded. New ones had formed. And it had felt natural at the time, not like loss.

"But this feels different," Sam insisted. "This feels like everything is ending."

"Or," her dad said gently, "it feels like everything is beginning."

Moving day came too fast. Sam said goodbye to Lily at the end of her driveway, both of them crying so hard they could barely speak.

"It's not goodbye," Lily said through tears. "It's see you later."

"See you later," Sam echoed, even though it felt like goodbye.

The drive to Boston took fourteen hours. Sam spent most of it staring out the window, watching her old life disappear mile by mile.

Their new house was nice. Bigger than their old one. But it didn't feel like home. It felt like a stranger's house that Sam was visiting.

Her new room had better light than her old one. A bigger closet. But it was empty. No posters on the walls. No memories in the corners. Just blank space waiting to be filled.

Sam didn't want to fill it. She wanted her old room back.

The first day at her new school was torture. Everyone already had friend groups. Everyone already knew each other. Sam sat alone at lunch, scrolling through pictures on her phone of her old life, feeling like a ghost haunting someone else's world.

"Is anyone sitting here?" A girl with dark curly hair and kind eyes gestured to the empty seat across from Sam.

"No, it's free."

The girl sat down, unpacking her lunch. "I'm Ava. You're new, right?"

"That obvious?"

"Only because I haven't seen you before, and I've been here since sixth grade." Ava smiled. "Where'd you move from?"

"Ohio."

"Long way from home. That must be hard."

Sam felt tears prick her eyes. Everyone else had asked where she was from with casual curiosity. Ava was the first person to acknowledge it might be difficult.

"It's the worst," Sam admitted. "Everything's different. I don't know anyone. I miss my friends. I miss my old life."

"Yeah, change sucks," Ava said simply. "But it gets easier. I know that probably doesn't help right now, but it's true."

"How would you know?"

"Because I moved here three years ago. From Atlanta. And I felt exactly how you're feeling now." Ava took a bite of her sandwich. "I thought I'd never adjust. I thought I'd be miserable forever. But then I met my best friend in art class. And I joined the drama club. And slowly, this place started to feel like home too."

"I don't want it to feel like home," Sam said. "That feels like betraying my old home."

Ava nodded thoughtfully. "I felt that way too. Like if I was happy here, it meant I was forgetting there. But that's not how it works. You can love multiple places. You can have a past and a present. They don't cancel each other out."

That night, Sam video called Lily like they'd promised. But it was awkward in a way it had never been before. They didn't know what to say. Their lives were already diverging.

Lily talked about things happening at school that Sam wasn't part of anymore. Sam tried to explain her new school but felt guilty, like talking about it was moving on.

After they hung up, Sam felt worse than before. The call was supposed to make her feel connected. Instead, it highlighted how much distance was already growing between them.

Her mom knocked on the door. "How was the call with Lily?"

"Weird. Wrong. I don't know." Sam sighed. "Everything's changing. Even us. And I hate it."

Her mom sat beside her. "Change is hard. It's uncomfortable and scary and sometimes it feels like loss. But Sam, change is also growth. You can't stay in one place forever, physically or emotionally. You have to let yourself move forward."

"But what if moving forward means losing what I had?"

"It might," her mom said honestly. "Some things from your old life won't survive the distance. That's painful but true. But other things will. The friendships that are meant to last will last. And you'll make new connections here too. Different ones, not better or worse, just different."

"I don't want different. I want what I had."

"I know, sweetheart. But what you had was beautiful because it was right for that time in your life. Now you're in a different time. And new things will be beautiful too, if you let them."

Slowly, reluctantly, Sam started letting herself adjust. She joined the school newspaper because Ava suggested it. She discovered a amazing bookstore two blocks from her house. She found a coffee shop with the best hot chocolate she'd ever tasted.

She texted Lily less frequently, not because she cared less, but because their lives were moving at different speeds now. And that was okay. Sad, but okay.

Three months into the school year, Sam was editing an article for the newspaper when she realized something. She'd gone the whole day without thinking about Ohio. Not because she'd forgotten, but because she'd been too busy living.

"You seem happier," Ava observed, looking over her shoulder at the article. "Not like, happy happy, but less miserable."

"I think I'm adjusting," Sam admitted. "I still miss home. But this place is starting to feel less foreign."

"That's how it happens. Little by little. One day you wake up and realize you've built a life here too."

Sam thought about that. A life here too. Not instead of, but in addition to. Both could exist.

During winter break, Sam flew back to Ohio to visit Lily. She was so excited she could barely contain herself. Finally, things would feel normal again. Finally, she'd be home.

But when she got there, something was off. Her old house had new people living in it, and seeing strangers in her bedroom window felt surreal. The town looked smaller than she remembered. And when she hung out with Lily, there were these weird gaps in conversation, inside jokes Sam didn't understand, references to people and events she hadn't been part of.

"It's weird," Lily said on Sam's last night there. "You being here but not really being here. You know?"

"Yeah," Sam said quietly. "I know."

"You're different too," Lily continued, not unkindly. "Like, you're still you. But there's something new about you. More confident, maybe. Or just... different."

Sam realized Lily was right. She had changed. Boston had changed her. New experiences had shaped her. She wasn't the same person who'd left six months ago.

"Is that bad?" Sam asked.

"No," Lily smiled. "It's just change. And change is okay."

On the plane back to Boston, Sam looked out the window at the clouds below. She'd spent so long fighting change, trying to hold onto the past, that she'd almost missed the present.

But she was done fighting now. She was ready to let herself flow with the change instead of against it.

When the plane landed and she saw her parents waiting at the airport, Sam realized something. She was happy to see them. Happy to be back. Not back home, but back to her new home.

Both places could be home. Both versions of herself could exist. The girl she was and the girl she was becoming.

At school on Monday, Ava asked how the trip was.

"Good," Sam said. "Strange, but good. It made me realize something."

"What's that?"

"I spent so long being angry about change that I forgot change is just life happening. You can't stop it. You can't freeze time. All you can do is adapt and find the beauty in whatever comes next."

"Look at you, getting all philosophical," Ava teased.

"I'm serious though. I thought change was the enemy. But it's not. It's just... the only constant. Everything changes. People, places, feelings. And that's not bad. It's just true."

"So you're okay now? With the move?"

Sam thought about it. "I'm getting there. I still miss Ohio sometimes. I still miss what I had. But I'm also grateful for what I have now. For this school, for the newspaper, for you. I wouldn't have any of this if I hadn't moved."

"Life's weird like that," Ava said. "Sometimes the things we fight hardest against turn out to be exactly what we needed."

That night, Sam started a new journal entry. She'd been documenting the move since the beginning, mostly angry rants about how unfair everything was.

But tonight, she wrote something different.

"Change used to terrify me. It felt like loss, like endings, like everything I loved slipping away. But I'm learning that change isn't the opposite of stability. It's the path to growth. Yes, I lost things when I moved. But I also gained things. New friends. New experiences. New parts of myself I didn't know existed.

The old me would have fought this forever. Would have held onto the past so tightly she missed the present. But the new me? She's learning to let go. To adapt. To find home wherever she plants her feet.

Because the truth is, change is the only constant. And fighting it just makes you tired. Better to flow with it. To trust that even when it's uncomfortable, even when it hurts, it's leading you somewhere you need to go.

I'm not the same girl who left Ohio. And that's okay. That girl was great. But this girl? She's great too. Just different. Changed.

And change, I'm learning, is just another word for growth."

Reflect & Grow

Questions for you:

- What changes in your life have you resisted? Looking back, did those changes teach you anything valuable?
- How do you typically react to change? Do you embrace it or fight against it? Why?
- Think of a difficult transition you've been through. What did you learn about yourself during that time?

- What would it feel like to stop fighting change and start flowing with it?

Remember: Change is inevitable. Fighting it is like fighting the tide - exhausting and ultimately futile. But accepting change doesn't mean you can't grieve what you're losing. It just means you're also open to what you might gain. Every ending is also a beginning. Every goodbye makes room for a new hello. You don't have to like change. You just have to let it happen, trust that you'll adapt, and believe that whatever comes next has something to teach you.

True Friendship Shows Up in the Storm

Kennedy Walsh had 847 followers on Instagram and three "best friends" who she hung out with every single day.

She thought she had it all figured out.

Then her dad lost his job.

At first, Kennedy didn't tell anyone. It was embarrassing. Her family had always been comfortable, upper-middle-class, the kind of people who went on beach vacations every summer and never worried about money.

But now her dad was home all day in sweatpants, and her mom was stressed, and there were hushed conversations about budgets and cutting back.

"We might need to sell the house," Kennedy overheard her mom say one night. "Move somewhere smaller. More affordable."

Kennedy felt sick. Their house was in the best neighborhood. All her friends lived nearby. What would they think if she had to move to a cheaper area?

More importantly, what would they think of her?

Kennedy tried to keep everything normal. She still went to the mall with her friends, even though she couldn't actually buy anything. She still posted pictures that made her life look perfect. She still laughed and smiled and pretended everything was fine.

"Want to go to that new restaurant downtown this weekend?" her friend Madison asked at lunch. "I heard it's amazing but super expensive."

Kennedy's stomach twisted. "I can't. I'm... busy."

"Again? You've been 'busy' like three weekends in a row." Madison's eyes narrowed. "Is everything okay?"

"Everything's fine," Kennedy said quickly. "Just family stuff."

Her other friends, Brooke and Taylor, exchanged glances but didn't push.

Things got worse. Kennedy's family cancelled their summer beach trip. They cut cable. Her mom started buying generic brands instead of name brands. Small changes that felt enormous to Kennedy.

At school, her friends planned a spring break trip to Miami.

"It's going to be incredible," Brooke gushed, showing Kennedy pictures of the hotel. "Our parents are splitting the cost. It's only like $800 per person for the whole week!"

Only $800. Kennedy used to think that was nothing. Now it might as well be a million dollars.

"I don't think I can go," Kennedy said quietly.

"What? Why not?" Taylor looked genuinely confused.

Kennedy wanted to tell the truth. That her family couldn't afford it. That everything had changed. But the words stuck in her throat. What if they pitied her? What if they saw her differently? What if they didn't want to be friends with her anymore?

"I just... my parents won't let me. Family trip that week," she lied.

"That sucks," Madison said, already losing interest. "Well, we'll take lots of pictures for you."

Kennedy smiled like it was fine. Like she wasn't dying inside.

There was one person Kennedy didn't hang out with much anymore. Zara Patel had been her best friend in middle school, before Kennedy had gotten "cool" and started hanging out with Madison's group.

Zara was smart, funny, and didn't care about being popular. She wore thrift store clothes and brought homemade lunches and never seemed to worry about what people thought of her.

Kennedy had slowly drifted away from her, choosing parties and mall trips over Zara's book club and movie nights.

But one day, Zara found Kennedy crying in the bathroom during lunch.

"Kennedy? What's wrong?"

Kennedy quickly wiped her eyes. "Nothing. I'm fine."

Zara leaned against the sink, not buying it. "You're not fine. You've been weird for weeks. What's going on?"

And suddenly, Kennedy couldn't hold it in anymore. The whole story came pouring out. Her dad's job loss. The money problems. The lies she'd been telling. The fear of losing her friends if they knew the truth.

"I can't even afford to go on the Miami trip," Kennedy said, her voice breaking. "And I can't tell them why because what if they think I'm... less than them now?"

Zara was quiet for a moment. Then she said, "If they think less of you because your family is going through a hard time, they're not real friends."

"But they're all I have."

"Are they though? Or are they just people you hang out with when everything's easy?" Zara's voice was gentle but firm. "Real friends don't disappear when things get hard, Kennedy. They show up."

That weekend, Kennedy stayed home while her friends went to a concert she couldn't afford. She posted that she was sick to avoid explaining.

Sunday afternoon, her doorbell rang. It was Zara, holding a bag of popcorn and a stack of movies.

"What are you doing here?" Kennedy asked, surprised.

"You said you were sick. I brought comfort supplies." Zara walked past her into the house. "Also, I figured you might want company."

"I'm not actually sick," Kennedy admitted.

"I know. You couldn't afford the concert." Zara said it matter-of-factly, without judgment. "So I brought the entertainment to you."

They spent the afternoon watching movies and talking, really talking, in a way Kennedy hadn't with anyone in months. Zara didn't ask for explanations or make Kennedy feel ashamed. She just showed up.

"Why are you being so nice to me?" Kennedy asked. "I kind of ditched you when I started hanging out with Madison's group."

"I know," Zara said. "That hurt. But you're still my friend. And friends show up when things are hard, not just when they're easy."

Monday at school, Madison confronted Kennedy at her locker.

"Why did Zara post a picture of you guys watching movies yesterday? I thought you were sick."

Kennedy's cheeks burned. She'd been caught in her lie.

"I wasn't actually sick," she admitted quietly.

"So you lied to us? Why?"

This was it. The moment Kennedy had been dreading. She could lie again, make up another excuse. Or she could tell the truth and risk everything.

Kennedy took a deep breath. "Because I couldn't afford the concert. My dad lost his job and we're having money problems and I've been too embarrassed to tell you."

Madison blinked. "Wait, seriously?"

"Yeah. We might have to move. We're cutting back on everything. I can't do the Miami trip or expensive restaurants or shopping at the mall. And I thought if you knew, you wouldn't want to be friends with me anymore."

There was a long pause. Then Madison said, "Kennedy, that's literally insane. Why would we care about that?"

"Because money is kind of your thing," Kennedy said honestly. "All we ever do is spend money. Shop, eat out, concerts. If I can't do those things, what do we even have in common?"

Madison looked uncomfortable. "I mean... I guess we do spend a lot. But we're friends because we like hanging out, not because of money."

"Are we though?" Kennedy asked softly. "Because when I told you I couldn't go to Miami, you just said you'd take pictures for me and moved on. You didn't ask why. You didn't seem to care."

"I thought you just didn't want to go," Madison said defensively.

"Because I made it easy for you to think that. I lied rather than risk you knowing the truth." Kennedy closed her locker. "But Zara knew something was wrong. She showed up. She asked questions. She cared enough to dig deeper."

Madison was quiet for a moment. Then she said, "So you're saying we're not good friends."

"I'm saying I don't know if we're real friends. Fair-weather friends, maybe. But when things got hard, none of you noticed I was drowning."

At lunch, Kennedy sat with Zara. Madison, Brooke, and Taylor kept glancing over, whispering among themselves.

"You okay?" Zara asked.

"I don't know. I might have just ended all my friendships."

"Maybe. Or maybe you just figured out which ones were real."

After lunch, Brooke approached Kennedy alone.

"Hey. Can we talk?"

They went outside to the courtyard. Brooke sat on a bench, patting the spot next to her.

"Madison told us what you said. About your dad and the money stuff." Brooke's voice was softer than usual. "I'm really sorry you're going through that. And I'm sorry we didn't notice."

"It's not your fault. I hid it."

"Yeah, but we should have seen something was off. Madison's right that we spend a lot. We kind of made friendship about money without realizing it." Brooke picked at her nail polish. "My parents got divorced last year. It was really messy. And I didn't tell anyone because I was embarrassed. I just kept pretending everything was fine. So I get it. The hiding, the fear of being seen differently."

Kennedy looked at her, surprised. "I didn't know that."

"Because I didn't tell anyone. Not even you guys. We're all so busy showing our highlight reels that we forget to be real with each other." Brooke took a breath. "I want to be better at this. At being a real friend, not just someone you hang out with when things are fun."

"I want that too," Kennedy said.

"So maybe we start over? Do stuff that doesn't cost money? Just actually hang out and talk and be there for each other?"

Kennedy smiled. "I'd like that."

Over the next few weeks, things shifted. Madison and Taylor slowly faded from Kennedy's daily life. They weren't mean about it, just distant. Without the shopping and expensive outings, they didn't really have much to connect over.

But Brooke stuck around. She started suggesting free activities - hiking, movie nights at home, studying at the library. She asked how Kennedy's dad's job search was going. She showed up.

And Zara? Zara had been there all along, waiting for Kennedy to realize what she'd walked away from.

One Friday night, the three of them were having a movie night at Zara's house when Brooke's phone buzzed.

"It's Madison. They're at that new club downtown and want to know if we want to come." Brooke looked at Kennedy. "It's probably expensive."

"You can go if you want," Kennedy said.

Brooke put her phone down. "Nah. I'm good here. This is more fun anyway."

And the thing was, it really was more fun. Laughing over inside jokes. Talking about real things. Being themselves without performing for an audience.

This, Kennedy realized, was what real friendship looked like. Not filtered photos and expensive outings, but showing up for each other when it mattered.

Months later, Kennedy's dad finally got a new job. It paid less than his old one, and things were still tight, but the crisis had passed. They didn't have to move after all.

At school, Madison approached Kennedy at her locker.

"Hey. I heard about your dad's new job. That's great."

"Thanks."

"Listen, I've been thinking about what you said. About fair-weather friends." Madison shifted uncomfortably. "You were right. I wasn't there for you when things got hard. And I'm sorry."

"I appreciate that," Kennedy said.

"I'm not saying we have to be best friends or whatever. But maybe we could hang out sometime? Do something low-key?"

Kennedy thought about it. Madison wasn't a bad person. She just hadn't known how to be a real friend. But maybe she was trying to learn.

"Yeah," Kennedy said. "I'd like that."

That weekend, Zara, Brooke, and Kennedy went hiking at the state park. It was free, beautiful, and exactly where Kennedy wanted to be.

At the top of the trail, looking out over the valley, Brooke said, "You know what I realized? The best things in life really are free. Friends who actually care. Moments like this. Stuff that matters."

"That sounds like a Hallmark card," Zara teased.

"But it's true!" Brooke laughed. "Kennedy, I'm actually glad your family went through that hard time. Not because I wanted you to suffer, but because it showed me what real friendship looks like. It showed all of us."

Kennedy thought about the storm her family had weathered. The fear, the embarrassment, the uncertainty. It had been awful.

But it had also revealed the truth. Who showed up when things got hard. Who stayed when life wasn't Instagram-perfect. Who loved her for who she was, not what she could afford.

"True friendship shows up in the storm," Kennedy said quietly. "Not just on sunny days."

"Exactly," Zara said, linking her arm through Kennedy's. "And we're here for all the weather. Rain or shine."

Kennedy smiled, feeling lighter than she had in months. She'd lost followers and fair-weather friends. But she'd gained something so much more valuable.

She'd gained friends who showed up when it mattered. And that, she realized, was everything.

Reflect & Grow

Questions for you:

- Think about your friendships. Are they based on what you do together or who you truly are?
- Have you ever had a friend show up for you during a difficult time? How did that feel?
- Are you the kind of friend who shows up in the storm, or only on sunny days? Be honest.
- What's the difference between popularity and real friendship? Which one are you pursuing?

Remember: Fair-weather friends are everywhere. They're easy to find and fun to be around when life is good. But real friends? They're rare. They're the ones who notice when you're struggling, even when you try to hide it. They're the ones who show up with popcorn when you can't afford the concert. They're the ones who love you for who you are, not what you have or how you make them look. Quality over quantity. Always. A few real friends are worth more than hundreds of fake ones. Invest your energy in the friendships that show up in the storm, and let the fair-weather ones drift away.

Words Can Hurt or Heal

Olivia Martinez was known for being funny.

Sharp wit. Quick comebacks. The kind of humor that made people laugh and earned her a reputation as the class comedian.

But there was a fine line between funny and mean, and Olivia didn't always stay on the right side of it.

"Oh my God, did you see what Ashley wore today?" Olivia said at lunch, loud enough for several tables to hear. "It looks like her grandma's curtains exploded."

Her friends laughed. Olivia felt the familiar rush of satisfaction that came with making people laugh, with being clever, with being noticed.

She didn't see Ashley's face fall across the cafeteria. Didn't see her pull her cardigan tighter around herself. Didn't see her leave early, eyes shiny with tears.

Olivia didn't think about the impact of her words. They were just jokes. Just funny observations. No one was supposed to take them seriously.

That afternoon, Olivia's English teacher, Ms. Chen, asked her to stay after class.

"I wanted to talk to you about something," Ms. Chen said, sitting on the edge of her desk. "I overheard what you said about Ashley at lunch today."

Olivia's stomach tightened. "It was just a joke. I wasn't trying to be mean."

"Intent and impact aren't always the same thing," Ms. Chen said gently. "You might not have intended to hurt her. But your words did. Ashley left school early today, upset."

"I didn't know she heard it," Olivia said defensively.

"Does that matter? If someone gets hurt by your words, does it matter whether they heard them directly or they got back to them through someone else?"

Olivia didn't have an answer.

"Olivia, you're funny. You have this incredible ability to see things in clever ways and articulate them. That's a gift. But like any gift, it can be used to build people up or tear them down. Right now, you're using it to get laughs at other people's expense. Is that really who you want to be?"

The question sat heavy in Olivia's chest. She wanted to defend herself, to say it was all in good fun, to insist people were too sensitive. But something in Ms. Chen's words struck a nerve.

That night, Olivia couldn't stop thinking about Ashley. About the cardigan comment. About the way her friends had laughed.

She pulled out her phone and scrolled through her text messages. There were dozens of similar jokes. Comments about people's appearances, their choices, their quirks. Things she'd said to make her friends laugh.

Things that probably hurt people.

Olivia remembered something from years ago, back in sixth grade. A girl named Emma had called Olivia "chunky" in front of the whole class. Everyone had laughed. Olivia had laughed too, pretending it didn't bother her.

But she'd gone home and cried. She'd stared at herself in the mirror, wondering if everyone saw her that way. That one word had stuck with her for years.

And now she was doing the same thing to other people.

The next day, Olivia found Ashley by her locker.

"Hey," Olivia said, her voice smaller than usual. "Can I talk to you for a second?"

Ashley looked wary but nodded.

"I wanted to apologize for what I said yesterday. About your cardigan. It was mean and unnecessary and I'm really sorry."

Ashley's eyes widened slightly. "Oh. Um. Thanks."

"I'm serious. I have this thing where I go for the joke without thinking about how it affects people. And that's not okay. You didn't deserve that."

"It did hurt," Ashley admitted quietly. "I actually really like this cardigan. My grandma made it for me before she passed away last year."

Olivia felt like she'd been punched in the stomach. "Ashley, I'm so sorry. I had no idea."

"How could you? You didn't ask. You just saw something you could make fun of and went for it." Ashley's voice wasn't angry, just tired. "You do that a lot, Olivia. Make jokes at people's expense. Maybe you think it's harmless, but it's not. Words stick with people."

Olivia nodded, feeling tears prick her eyes. "You're right. I'm going to do better. I promise."

Doing better was harder than Olivia expected. Her default mode was sarcasm and quick jabs. Holding back felt like swallowing words that wanted to come out.

At lunch, her friend Jessica pointed at a guy across the cafeteria. "Oh my God, look at Marcus's haircut. What was he thinking?"

Everyone turned to look. Olivia opened her mouth, a perfect joke ready on her tongue about Marcus looking like he'd lost a fight with a lawnmower.

But then she remembered Ashley's face. The cardigan her grandmother had made. The weight of careless words.

"Actually, I think it looks good," Olivia said instead. "Takes confidence to try a new style."

Her friends stared at her like she'd grown a second head.

"Are you feeling okay?" Jessica asked, half-joking.

"I'm fine. Just tired of being mean for laughs."

Later, Marcus walked past their table. On impulse, Olivia called out, "Hey, Marcus. Cool haircut."

He looked surprised but pleased. "Really? Thanks!"

It was a small moment. But it felt different than making people laugh at his expense. Better, somehow.

Over the next few weeks, Olivia started paying attention to her words. Really paying attention. She realized how often she'd used humor as a weapon, hiding cruelty behind the excuse of "just joking."

She also started using her words differently. When her friend Tara was nervous about a presentation, instead of making a joke about her stuttering, Olivia said, "You've got this. You know your stuff."

When a freshman dropped their tray in the cafeteria and everyone laughed, Olivia helped them clean it up and said, "Happens to everyone. Don't worry about it."

Small words. But they mattered.

One day, a new girl named Priya joined their class. She was shy, wore traditional Indian clothes sometimes, and spoke with an accent.

Jessica immediately started whispering jokes to Olivia. "I can't understand half of what she says. And what is she wearing? Is that a costume?"

The old Olivia would have joined in. Would have added her own observations, made everyone laugh, been clever at someone else's expense.

But the new Olivia remembered being called "chunky" in sixth grade. Remembered Ashley's grandmother's cardigan. Remembered that words stick with people.

"Actually, I think her clothes are beautiful," Olivia said loudly enough for Priya to hear. "Way more interesting than what we wear."

Priya looked up, surprised. She smiled at Olivia, a small, grateful smile.

Jessica rolled her eyes. "Since when did you become so sensitive?"

"I'm not being sensitive. I'm just not being cruel anymore." Olivia met her friend's eyes. "There's a difference between being funny and being mean. I'm learning to stay on the right side of that line."

In English class, Ms. Chen assigned a creative writing piece about the power of language. Olivia wrote about her journey from using words as weapons to using them as tools for kindness.

"I used to think being funny meant making people laugh, no matter the cost," she wrote. "But laughter at someone else's pain isn't real humor. It's just cruelty with an audience. Real wit doesn't punch down. It doesn't make people feel small to make yourself feel big. I'm learning that the most powerful thing you can do with words is use them to make someone's day better, not worse."

Ms. Chen gave her an A and wrote at the top: "I'm proud of your growth."

A month after her conversation with Ashley, Olivia was walking home from school when she saw Ashley sitting on a bench, crying.

"Hey," Olivia said, sitting down beside her. "What's wrong?"

"Nothing. Everything. I don't know." Ashley wiped her eyes. "My mom and I got in a huge fight. She doesn't understand me. Nobody does."

"That sounds really hard," Olivia said. "Want to talk about it?"

They sat there for an hour, Olivia mostly listening as Ashley talked about her family, her insecurities, her fears. Olivia didn't make jokes or try to fix anything. She just listened and said things like "that makes sense" and "you're not alone in feeling that way."

When they finally stood up to leave, Ashley hugged her.

"Thank you," Ashley said. "I didn't think we were friends, after... everything. But you really helped today."

"I want to be your friend," Olivia said. "If you'll let me. The real kind of friend who builds you up instead of tearing you down."

"I'd like that."

Olivia's humor didn't disappear. She was still funny, still quick with observations and clever turns of phrase. But now she aimed her wit at situations, not people. At absurdities, not insecurities. She made people laugh with her, not at someone else.

And she discovered something surprising. This kind of humor was better. It felt cleaner. It didn't leave a bitter aftertaste or a nagging guilt.

One day, a freshman was getting picked on in the hallway. A group of older kids were making fun of his glasses, calling him names, laughing.

The old Olivia might have joined in or walked past. But this Olivia stopped.

"Hey, guys. Don't you have anything better to do than pick on someone half your size?"

"Chill, Olivia. We're just joking around."

"Jokes are supposed to be funny for everyone, including the person you're joking about. This is just being a jerk." She looked at the freshman. "Come on, I'll walk with you."

As they walked away, the boy said quietly, "Thanks. That was brave."

"Not really," Olivia said. "Just basic decency. But I appreciate it."

At the end of the year, the school did "senior superlatives" where students voted on different categories. Olivia had always imagined winning "Class Clown" or "Funniest."

She won "Kindest."

When they announced it at the senior assembly, Olivia felt tears in her eyes. Six months ago, no one would have called her kind. She'd been funny, yes. Popular, maybe. But kind? Never.

After the assembly, Ashley found her in the hallway.

"Congratulations," Ashley said, smiling. "You deserve it."

"I don't know about that. I spent most of high school being the opposite of kind."

"But you changed. That's what matters. You showed everyone that it's never too late to become a better version of yourself."

Olivia thought about that. About the words she used to throw around carelessly. About the people she'd hurt. About the person she'd been and the person she was becoming.

Words could hurt. She'd proven that over and over. But words could also heal. Could build up instead of tear down. Could make someone's day instead of ruining it.

And that was a power worth using wisely.

On graduation day, Olivia gave a speech as part of the senior class council. She talked about growth, about learning from mistakes, about the impact of our words.

"We all have power," she said, looking out at her classmates. "The power to hurt or the power to heal. The power to tear down or to build up. Our words are tools, and we get to choose how we use them. I spent too long using mine as weapons. I'm spending the rest of my life using them as bridges. I hope you'll join me."

As she walked off the stage, she saw Ashley in the crowd, wearing her grandmother's cardigan and clapping.

Olivia smiled. Words had gotten her into trouble. But they'd also given her a chance to make things right.

And that, she realized, was the real power of language. Not just the ability to wound, but the ability to heal. To apologize. To change. To choose, every single day, what kind of impact you want to have on the world.

One word at a time.

Reflect & Grow

Questions for you:

- Think about the words you use most often. Do they build people up or tear them down?
- Have you ever hurt someone with your words, even if you didn't mean to? How did you handle it?

- Can you remember a time when someone's words really affected you, positively or negatively? What did that teach you?
- What would change if you started using your words to heal instead of hurt?

Remember: Words are powerful. They can wound or heal, destroy or build, hurt or help. And once they're out there, you can't take them back. "Just joking" doesn't erase the pain they cause. Being funny isn't worth making someone feel small. The most courageous thing you can do with your words is use them to lift others up, to speak truth with kindness, to choose compassion over cruelty. Every word you speak is a choice. Choose wisely. Choose kindness. Choose to be someone whose words make the world a little bit better.

Judging Is Easy, Understanding Takes Courage

H arper Williams knew everything about everyone at Lincoln High.

Or at least, she thought she did.

There was Jake Morrison, the jock who probably couldn't spell his own name. There was Melissa Chen, the try-hard who raised her hand for every question. There was Danny Foster, the weird kid who ate lunch alone and wore the same hoodie every day.

Harper had everyone figured out, placed neatly in boxes with labels. It made the world simpler, more predictable.

She never thought about what might be inside those boxes. The stories behind the labels. The complexity hidden beneath the surface.

Until she got partnered with Danny Foster for the biggest project of the semester.

"You've got to be kidding me," Harper muttered when Mrs. Patterson announced the partners.

Danny sat three rows away, hood up as always, not making eye contact with anyone. He hadn't said a word all semester except when forced to by teachers.

After class, Harper approached him reluctantly. "So, I guess we should figure out when to work on this project."

Danny shrugged, still not looking at her. "Whatever works for you."

"Can you at least try to care? This is worth 30% of our grade."

"I care." His voice was quiet but sharp. "I just don't need to perform enthusiasm about it."

Harper rolled her eyes. This was going to be a disaster.

They agreed to meet at the library after school. Harper arrived on time with a detailed outline she'd already created. Danny arrived ten minutes late, still wearing that same ratty hoodie.

"Where were you?" Harper demanded.

"Had something to take care of." He sat down and pulled out a beat-up notebook. "What's the plan?"

Harper slid her outline across the table. "I already did most of the planning. You can just follow this."

Danny looked at the paper, then at her. "Did you even ask what I think we should do?"

"I assumed you wouldn't have ideas."

"You assumed wrong." He pulled out his own notebook, filled with detailed notes and sketches. "I was thinking we could approach it from this angle instead."

Harper stared at his notes. They were good. Really good. More creative and thorough than her own outline.

"I thought you didn't care about school," she said.

"You don't know anything about me," Danny said flatly. "You just decided who I was based on... what? That I wear a hoodie and don't talk much?"

Harper felt her cheeks burn. He was right. She had made assumptions. Unfair ones.

Over the next week, they met several times to work on the project. Harper started noticing things she'd missed before.

Danny was smart. Not just smart, but brilliant. He saw connections between ideas that Harper never would have thought of. He was creative, thoughtful, and actually really funny in a dry, unexpected way.

One afternoon, Harper's curiosity got the better of her.

"Can I ask you something? Why do you always eat alone? Why don't you talk to people?"

Danny was quiet for a long moment. "Because I'm tired."

"Tired of what?"

"Of performing. Of pretending to be whoever people want me to be. Of small talk and fake friendships and all the energy it takes to be 'normal.'" He looked at her directly for the first time. "I have enough going on at home. School is the one place I can just exist without having to be anything for anyone."

"What do you mean, at home?"

Danny hesitated, then said quietly, "My mom has MS. Multiple sclerosis. Some days she's okay. Some days she can't get out of bed. I help take care of her before and after school. That's why I'm always late, why I'm always tired, why I don't have energy for social performance."

Harper felt like the floor had dropped out from under her. "I had no idea."

"Of course you didn't. Nobody does. Because nobody asks. They just see a quiet kid in a hoodie and make up stories about who I must be."

That night, Harper couldn't stop thinking about Danny. About all the assumptions she'd made. About how wrong she'd been.

She thought about other people too. Jake Morrison, the jock she'd dismissed as dumb. Did she actually know anything about him? Melissa Chen, the try-hard. Maybe she was just passionate about learning. Had Harper ever considered that?

She'd spent so much time judging people, putting them in boxes, that she'd never bothered to actually see them.

The next day, Harper did something she'd never done before. She sat with Danny at lunch.

"What are you doing?" he asked, looking uncomfortable.

"Sitting with my project partner. Is that okay?"

"People are going to think you're weird."

"Let them." Harper unwrapped her sandwich. "I was thinking about what you said. About how nobody asks. So I'm asking. Tell me about your mom. What's it like?"

Danny looked at her warily, like he was trying to figure out if this was some kind of trick. Then, slowly, he started talking.

He told her about his mom's diagnosis three years ago. About how some days were good and some were devastating. About how he'd learned to cook and clean and help with physical therapy. About how exhausting it was but also how it had changed him, made him grow up faster than his peers.

"That's why I wear the same hoodie," he admitted. "It was my dad's. He left when my mom got sick. Couldn't handle it. The hoodie is like... I don't know. Armor, I guess."

"I'm sorry," Harper said. "About your dad. About everything."

"I don't want pity. I just want people to not assume they know my story without asking."

Harper started seeing the school differently after that. She watched people with new eyes, wondering what stories they carried that nobody knew about.

Jake Morrison stayed after class to ask the teacher for extra help. Not because he was dumb, but because he cared about getting better.

Melissa Chen raised her hand constantly not to show off, but because she genuinely loved learning and got excited about ideas.

The quiet girl in Harper's math class who never talked? She was dealing with severe social anxiety, working with a therapist to manage it.

Everyone had a story. Everyone was fighting battles that weren't visible on the surface.

And Harper had been so busy judging that she'd missed all of it.

For their project presentation, Harper insisted that Danny take the lead. He was hesitant at first, but when he started talking, his passion for the subject came through. He was engaging, articulate, brilliant.

After the presentation, several classmates approached him with questions, genuinely interested in what he had to say. Harper watched Danny's surprise, then his slow smile as he realized people were actually listening.

"That was amazing," Harper told him afterward. "You're really talented."

"Thanks for letting me do it," Danny said. "I know public speaking isn't your favorite either."

"How did you know that?"

"Because I pay attention. You always look nervous before presentations. Your hands shake a little. But you push through anyway." He smiled. "People are more complex than they seem. You taught me that it's worth the risk to let people see you. So thanks."

A week later, Harper was in the cafeteria when she overheard two girls gossiping.

"Did you see Harper sitting with Danny Foster? What is she thinking? That guy is so weird."

"I know, right? He never talks to anyone. Probably doesn't have any friends for a reason."

The old Harper might have agreed with them. Might have defended herself, distanced from Danny, protected her own reputation.

But the new Harper, the one who'd learned that judging is easy but understanding takes courage, did something different.

"Actually," Harper said, turning to face them, "Danny is one of the most interesting people I've met. He's smart, funny, and dealing with stuff you couldn't imagine. Maybe instead of judging him for being quiet, you could try being curious about why."

The girls looked embarrassed and quickly changed the subject.

Danny, who'd overheard the whole thing, caught Harper's eye from across the cafeteria. He nodded once, a small gesture of appreciation.

Harper started actively challenging her own judgments. Every time she caught herself making an assumption about someone, she stopped and asked herself: Do I actually know this? Or am I just guessing?

More often than not, she was just guessing.

She started conversations with people she'd previously dismissed. She asked questions. She listened to stories.

She discovered that the girl with the designer clothes was working two jobs to afford them because fashion was her passion. The guy who seemed arrogant was actually deeply insecure and used confidence as a shield. The teacher everyone called strict had lost her own daughter to bullying and was trying to create a safer environment.

Everyone had depth. Everyone had reasons.

At the end of the semester, Harper wrote an essay for English class titled "The Courage to Understand."

She wrote about Danny, about her own assumptions, about what she'd learned.

"Judging is easy," she wrote. "It takes seconds to look at someone and decide who they are based on surface-level observations. Understanding is harder. It requires curiosity, empathy, vulnerability, and time. It requires admitting that we don't know everything about everyone. It requires the courage to ask questions, to listen to answers, and to change our minds when we're wrong.

I spent years judging people from a distance, creating stories about who they were without ever talking to them. I thought I was protecting myself from disappointment or wasting time on people who didn't matter. But what I was really doing was missing out on connections, on stories, on the beautiful complexity of human beings.

Everyone is fighting a battle we know nothing about. Everyone has depths we can't see from the surface. And everyone deserves to be understood, not judged."

Her teacher wrote at the top: "This is your best work all year. Thank you for your honesty."

On the last day of school, Danny found Harper by her locker.

"Hey. I wanted to give you something." He handed her a folded piece of paper.

Harper opened it. It was a drawing of her, sketched in pencil, sitting in the library. She looked thoughtful, concentrated, real.

"I didn't know you could draw," Harper said, amazed.

"There's a lot you don't know about me," Danny said with a small smile. "But you're the first person who bothered to ask. Who took the time to understand instead of just judge. That meant everything to me."

"You changed how I see people," Harper admitted. "You showed me that everyone's more than what they seem."

"You changed how I see myself," Danny said. "You reminded me that I'm worth knowing. So thank you."

They hugged, an unlikely friendship that never would have happened if Harper hadn't learned the difference between judging and understanding.

That summer, Harper worked on really seeing people. Strangers at the coffee shop. Family members. People she'd known for years but never really understood.

She asked questions. She listened to stories. She suspended judgment and opened herself to curiosity.

And what she found was remarkable. Every single person, when given the chance, revealed layers of complexity and beauty she never would have discovered through judgment alone.

Her mom, who she'd always thought was just old-fashioned, had wanted to be an artist but gave it up to support the family. Her younger brother, who annoyed her constantly, was struggling with ADHD and doing his best. The barista at her favorite coffee shop was putting herself through college and sending money home to her family in another country.

Stories everywhere. Humanity everywhere. If only you had the courage to look past the surface and ask.

Judging was easy. It required nothing. Understanding took courage, time, and humility.

But the connections it created, the world it revealed, made it worth every bit of effort.

Harper had spent seventeen years judging. She'd spend the rest of her life understanding.

And that, she realized, would make all the difference.

Reflect & Grow

Questions for you:

- Think of someone you've judged without really knowing. What assumptions did you make? Are you sure they're true?
- What stops you from asking questions and trying to understand people instead of judging them?
- Have you ever been judged unfairly? How did it feel? Did it make you want to judge others less?
- What would your school, your friendships, your world look like if everyone chose understanding over judgment?

Remember: Everyone you meet is fighting a battle you know nothing about. Everyone has a story more complex than what you see on the surface. Judging is quick and easy, but it keeps you from real connection. Understanding takes courage, time, and genuine curiosity, but it opens doors to empathy, growth, and authentic relationships. The next time you catch yourself judging someone, pause. Ask a question instead. Listen to the answer. Choose curiosity over assumption. Choose understanding over judgment. You might be surprised by what you discover.

Forgiveness Frees You, Not Just Them

Natalie Kim hadn't spoken to her former best friend in exactly 437 days.

Not that she was counting.

Okay, she was totally counting.

It had been 437 days since Sophie betrayed her. Since Sophie told everyone Natalie's biggest secret. Since their friendship exploded in the worst possible way.

And Natalie was still angry. Furiously, constantly, exhaustingly angry.

"You need to let it go," her older sister Claire said, watching Natalie glare at Sophie across the cafeteria for the millionth time. "This grudge is eating you alive."

"She doesn't deserve forgiveness," Natalie shot back. "Do you know what she did to me?"

"I know. But holding onto anger is like drinking poison and expecting the other person to die. You're the one suffering here, not her."

Natalie wanted to argue, but she couldn't. Because Claire was right. Sophie seemed fine. She had new friends, she laughed in the hallways, she looked happy.

Meanwhile, Natalie couldn't get through a single day without thinking about the betrayal. It consumed her. Defined her. Held her hostage.

Natalie and Sophie had been best friends since third grade. Inseparable. The kind of friends who knew everything about each other, who finished each other's sentences, who'd planned their futures together.

Then freshman year, Natalie told Sophie something she'd never told anyone else. Her parents were getting divorced, and her dad had been having an affair. Natalie was devastated, ashamed, scared.

She trusted Sophie with her deepest pain.

And Sophie, in a moment of careless gossip, told Jessica Martinez. Who told everyone else.

Within a week, the whole school knew. People whispered when Natalie walked by. They asked invasive questions. They treated her family drama like entertainment.

And Sophie, when confronted, had just said, "I didn't think it was that big a deal. Sorry."

Sorry. Like that fixed everything.

Natalie cut her off completely. Blocked her number. Refused to speak to her. And for 437 days, she'd held onto that anger like it was the only thing keeping her together.

In psychology class, Mr. Henderson started a unit on emotional health.

"Today we're talking about forgiveness," he said, writing the word on the board. "Not because people who hurt you deserve it, but because you deserve peace."

Natalie felt her jaw tighten.

"Forgiveness isn't about the other person," Mr. Henderson continued. "It's not about saying what they did was okay or excusing their behavior. It's about releasing yourself from the prison of resentment. Because when you hold a grudge, who suffers? You do. Every single day."

A girl in the back raised her hand. "But what if they don't deserve forgiveness? What if they never even apologized properly?"

"Forgiveness isn't about what they deserve. It's about what you need to be free." Mr. Henderson leaned against his desk. "Think of it this way. When you refuse to forgive someone, you're letting them live rent-free in your head. They might have moved on, but you're still giving them power over your peace. Is that really the revenge you want?"

Natalie stared at her desk, Mr. Henderson's words echoing in her mind.

That night, Natalie couldn't sleep. She kept thinking about the unit on forgiveness. About how much energy she'd spent being angry. About how Sophie probably didn't even think about her anymore while Natalie thought about Sophie constantly.

She grabbed her journal and started writing.

"I hate that I'm still so angry. I hate that she gets to be happy while I'm stuck in this loop of resentment. I hate that she took up so much space in my head for 437 days. But mostly, I hate that I can't seem to let it go.

Maybe Claire and Mr. Henderson are right. Maybe this anger is hurting me more than it's hurting her. Maybe I'm the one trapped, not her."

Natalie stared at what she'd written. The truth of it stung.

The next day, Natalie did something she hadn't done in over a year. She looked at Sophie's Instagram.

Sophie's life looked good. Really good. New friends. Lots of smiles. Zero evidence that she was suffering or thinking about Natalie at all.

Meanwhile, Natalie had been carrying this weight for 437 days. This anger that was supposed to punish Sophie but only punished herself.

It wasn't fair. But it was true.

In the library that afternoon, Natalie was studying when someone sat down across from her. She looked up.

It was Sophie.

"I know you don't want to talk to me," Sophie said quickly, before Natalie could leave. "But I need to say something. I've been trying to find the courage to tell you for months."

Natalie's first instinct was to walk away. But something made her stay.

"I'm so sorry," Sophie said, her voice breaking. "Not the shallow sorry I said before, but really, truly sorry. What I did was unforgivable. I betrayed your trust in the worst way. I was careless with your pain. And I've regretted it every single day since."

"You seemed pretty happy to me," Natalie said coldly.

"I'm good at pretending. But I lost my best friend, Natalie. You." Sophie wiped her eyes. "I know I don't deserve your forgiveness. I'm not asking for it. I just needed you to know that I'm sorry. That I understand what I did. That I wish I could take it back."

Natalie felt tears burning in her own eyes. "You can't take it back. The damage is done."

"I know. And I'll live with that. But you shouldn't have to. You shouldn't have to carry this anger around because of my mistake." Sophie stood up. "I just wanted you to know that I'm sorry. Really, deeply sorry. And I hope someday you can let go of this, not for me, but for yourself."

She walked away, leaving Natalie sitting there with her heart pounding.

That night at dinner, Natalie told her family about the encounter.

"Are you going to forgive her?" Claire asked.

"I don't know. Part of me wants to hold onto this anger. It feels like if I forgive her, I'm saying what she did was okay."

"Forgiveness doesn't mean that," her mom said gently. "It doesn't mean what she did was acceptable. It just means you're choosing not to let it define you anymore."

"But she hurt me so badly."

"I know, sweetheart. And that pain is valid. But think about it this way." Her mom reached across the table. "When your dad left, when I found out about the affair, I was so angry. I wanted to hold onto that anger forever. It felt justified. Earned."

This was the first time her mom had talked openly about the divorce since it happened.

"But the anger was destroying me," her mom continued. "Not him. Me. I wasn't sleeping. I was bitter. I was letting what he did control my present and my future. So I made a choice. I forgave him. Not because he deserved it, but because I deserved peace."

"How did you do it?"

"I stopped waiting for him to make it right. I stopped needing him to suffer as much as I was suffering. I released him from the debt I thought he owed me. And in doing that, I freed myself."

Over the next few weeks, Natalie thought a lot about forgiveness. About what it meant and what it didn't mean.

She realized she'd been holding Sophie hostage in her mind, replaying the betrayal over and over, keeping the wound fresh. And in doing that, she was also holding herself hostage.

The anger had become familiar. Comfortable, almost. A constant companion.

But it was also exhausting. Heavy. A weight she'd been carrying for 437 days that was crushing her.

What would it feel like to put it down?

One afternoon, Natalie saw Sophie sitting alone on a bench outside school, looking at her phone. Before she could overthink it, Natalie walked over.

"Can I sit?" Natalie asked.

Sophie looked up, shocked. "Yeah. Of course."

They sat in silence for a moment. Then Natalie said, "I've been thinking about what you said. About your apology."

"Natalie, I meant every word. I..."

"Let me finish." Natalie took a breath. "What you did really hurt me. It broke something between us that can't be fixed. And I'm not saying we're going to be best friends again or that everything is okay."

Sophie nodded, tears in her eyes.

"But I'm tired," Natalie continued. "I'm tired of being angry. I'm tired of giving you space in my head. I'm tired of carrying this weight. So I'm choosing to forgive you. Not because you deserve it, but because I do."

"Thank you," Sophie whispered. "I know we can't go back to how things were. But thank you."

"Forgiveness doesn't mean friendship," Natalie said firmly. "It just means I'm letting go of the anger. I'm releasing you from the debt I thought you owed me. I'm freeing myself."

"I understand. And that's more than I deserve."

They sat together for a few more minutes, a strange peace settling between them. It wasn't closure exactly. It was something different. Release, maybe.

That night, Natalie opened her journal and wrote:

"Day 438. The first day I'm not counting anymore.

I forgave Sophie today. Not because she earned it or because what she did was okay. I forgave her because I needed to be free.

I've spent over a year trapped in anger, replaying the betrayal, holding onto pain like it was protecting me from something. But it wasn't protecting me. It was poisoning me.

Forgiveness feels weird. Like I'm betraying myself somehow by letting her off the hook. But I'm learning that forgiveness isn't about letting her off the hook. It's about taking myself off the hook. Off the hook of constant anger, of reliving the pain, of giving her power over my peace.

She hurt me. That's true. That will always be true. But I don't have to let that hurt define the rest of my story.

I'm choosing peace over punishment. Freedom over resentment. My own wellbeing over revenge.

This doesn't mean we're friends again. This doesn't mean I trust her. This doesn't mean what she did was okay.

It just means I'm done carrying her mistake around with me everywhere I go.

I'm done counting the days since she betrayed me.

I'm ready to start counting the days I've been free."

A month later, Natalie realized she'd gone an entire week without thinking about Sophie. Without replaying the betrayal. Without feeling that familiar anger.

She felt lighter. Clearer. Like she'd been walking through water for over a year and suddenly found solid ground.

In psychology class, Mr. Henderson asked if anyone had thoughts on forgiveness to share.

Natalie raised her hand.

"I used to think forgiveness was about the other person," she said. "About whether they deserved it or earned it or apologized enough. But I learned it's actually about me. About choosing peace over anger. About deciding that my freedom is more important than their punishment."

"That's very insightful, Natalie," Mr. Henderson said. "What changed your mind?"

"I realized I was in prison. A prison of my own making, built from resentment and anger. And I was the only one with the key. Forgiveness was how I unlocked the door and walked out."

After class, a girl approached her. "That really resonated with me. I've been holding a grudge against someone for years. But hearing you talk about it being a prison... that's exactly what it feels like."

"So unlock the door," Natalie said. "Not for them. For you."

Sophie and Natalie never became close friends again. Some things, once broken, don't go back to how they were.

But they were cordial. They could exist in the same space without tension. They'd both moved on.

And more importantly, Natalie had moved on. The anger that had defined her for 437 days was gone. In its place was peace. Not happiness exactly, but something steadier. Something that felt like freedom.

She'd learned the hardest lesson about forgiveness. That it's not a gift you give to the person who hurt you. It's a gift you give to yourself.

And that gift, Natalie discovered, was priceless.

Reflect & Grow

Questions for you:

- Is there someone you're holding a grudge against? How is that anger affecting you? Is it affecting them?
- What does forgiveness mean to you? Have you been confusing it with excusing someone's behavior or reconciling with them?
- Think of a time someone forgave you. How did it feel? Did it change you?
- What would your life look like if you released yourself from the prison of resentment?

Remember: Forgiveness isn't about them. It's about you. It's not saying what they did was okay. It's saying you're done letting what they did control your peace. Holding onto anger is like gripping a hot coal with the intent of throwing it at someone else - you're the one who gets burned. Forgiveness is the moment you decide your freedom is more important than their punishment. It doesn't require reconciliation. It doesn't mean you have to trust them again. It just means you're releasing the debt you think they owe you and choosing peace instead. That's not weakness. That's the ultimate strength. The courage to free yourself.

Your Family Roots Are Hidden Treasure

J asmine Washington rolled her eyes as her grandmother launched into another story about "the old days."

"Back in Mississippi, when I was your age," Grandma Rose began, settling into her favorite chair, "we didn't have all these fancy phones and computers. We had to make our own entertainment."

Jasmine tuned out, scrolling through TikTok while her grandmother talked. She'd heard these stories a million times. They were boring, irrelevant, ancient history that had nothing to do with her life.

"Jasmine, are you even listening?" her mom asked, noticing her distraction.

"Sorry, Grandma. I have homework to do." Jasmine stood up, eager to escape.

She missed the hurt look on her grandmother's face.

At school, Jasmine's history teacher, Mr. Jackson, assigned a family heritage project.

"I want you to research your family history," he explained. "Interview relatives, look through old photos, create a presentation about where you came from. Due in three weeks."

Jasmine groaned. This sounded like torture. Who cared about dead people from a hundred years ago? What did that have to do with her life now?

Her friend Destiny leaned over. "This is going to be so boring. My grandparents are like, ancient. They don't understand anything about modern life."

"Same," Jasmine agreed. "My grandma is always talking about the past. Like, move on already."

But Mr. Jackson overheard. "The past isn't separate from the present, ladies. It's the foundation you're standing on. Whether you know it or not."

That weekend, Jasmine reluctantly asked her grandmother if they could talk for the project.

"Of course, baby!" Grandma Rose's face lit up. "What do you want to know?"

"Just like, basic stuff. Where you were born, when you came to Chicago, whatever." Jasmine pulled out her phone to record, treating it like a chore to check off.

"I was born in Greenwood, Mississippi in 1948," Grandma Rose began. "Things were very different then."

"Different how?" Jasmine asked, barely paying attention.

"Well, for one thing, I couldn't go to the same school as white children. Couldn't drink from the same water fountains. Couldn't sit at the front of the bus." Grandma Rose's voice was quiet but steady. "This was during segregation, baby. Jim Crow laws."

Jasmine looked up from her phone. She knew about segregation from history class, but hearing her own grandmother talk about living through it felt different somehow.

"That must have been hard," Jasmine said, actually listening now.

"Hard doesn't begin to cover it. But we survived. We persisted. We fought." Grandma Rose pulled out an old photo album. "See this? This is me at a sit-in in 1965. I was seventeen, just a bit older than you."

Jasmine stared at the black and white photo. A young woman who looked remarkably like her, sitting at a lunch counter, face determined despite the angry crowd behind her.

"You were part of the Civil Rights Movement?"

"We all were, in one way or another. We didn't have a choice. Change didn't come from sitting quietly. It came from standing up, speaking out, putting our bodies on the line." Grandma Rose touched the photo gently. "I got arrested that day. Spent two nights in jail. But we integrated that lunch counter."

"I had no idea," Jasmine whispered.

"Because you never asked, baby."

Over the next week, Jasmine kept coming back to talk to her grandmother. Each conversation revealed layers of history she'd never known.

Her grandmother had been the first in her family to graduate high school. She'd worked as a seamstress to put her own children through college. She'd marched with Dr. King. She'd survived poverty, racism, loss, and somehow emerged with her spirit intact.

"Why didn't you ever tell me these stories?" Jasmine asked.

"I've been telling you these stories your whole life, baby. You just weren't ready to hear them." Grandma Rose smiled sadly. "Young people always think the old folks are boring, that our stories don't matter. But our stories are your stories. Our strength is your inheritance."

Jasmine felt ashamed. All those times she'd tuned out, rolled her eyes, treated her grandmother's memories like they were worthless.

"Tell me more," Jasmine said. "Tell me everything."

Grandma Rose pulled out boxes of old photos, letters, documents. Each item had a story.

A ration card from World War II. A protest sign from a march. A letter from her own grandmother, written in careful cursive, describing the day she was freed from slavery.

"Wait, your grandmother was enslaved?" Jasmine felt dizzy. That wasn't ancient history. That was three generations ago.

"She was born enslaved in 1862. Freed when she was three years old. She lived until I was ten. I knew her, talked to her, heard her stories." Grandma Rose's eyes were distant. "She told me about being separated from her mother at auction. About learning to read in secret. About walking hundreds of miles to find her family after emancipation."

Jasmine's eyes filled with tears. "I can't imagine."

"You carry her strength in you. Her resilience. Her courage. That's what I'm trying to tell you, baby. You're not just Jasmine Washington, teenager with a phone. You're the culmination of generations of fighters, survivors, dreamers. Their blood runs in your veins. Their stories live in your bones."

For her project, Jasmine created a presentation that was nothing like what she'd originally planned. Instead of a boring slideshow of dates and names, she created a multimedia narrative.

She included photos of her great-great-grandmother. Audio clips of her grandmother's stories. Scanned images of historical documents. She traced her family's journey from slavery to segregation to the present day.

But more than facts, she included feelings. Reflections on what it meant to discover this history. Questions about identity and inheritance.

"I used to think my family's past was irrelevant," Jasmine wrote in her artist's statement. "Old stories from old people about old times. But I was wrong. My family's past is my foundation. It explains who I am and where I come from. It shows me that I'm part of something bigger than myself. That I carry the strength of people who survived the unsurvivable. That I have a responsibility to honor their struggles by living my life fully, by fighting for justice, by never taking for granted the freedoms they fought for."

On presentation day, Jasmine's project was last. By the time she finished, half the class was crying, including Mr. Jackson.

"That was extraordinary, Jasmine," he said, his voice thick. "Thank you for sharing your family's story with us."

After class, several students approached her.

"I had no idea your family went through all that," Destiny said. "That was so powerful."

"Thanks. I had no idea either until I actually listened to my grandmother." Jasmine packed up her materials. "I've been taking her for granted my whole life. Acting like her stories were boring. But they're not boring. They're treasure."

That night, Jasmine showed her grandmother the presentation.

They sat together on the couch, Grandma Rose holding Jasmine's hand as they watched the slideshow, listened to the audio clips, read the reflections.

When it ended, Grandma Rose was crying.

"Did I get something wrong?" Jasmine asked, worried.

"No, baby. You got it exactly right." Grandma Rose pulled her into a hug. "I've been trying to pass these stories to you for years. I was starting to think they'd die with me. But now I know they'll live on. You'll carry them forward."

"I will," Jasmine promised. "And I'll tell them to my kids someday. I'll make sure they know where they come from."

"That's all I've ever wanted. For you to know your roots. To understand that you're part of a long line of strong women who refused to give up. That strength is your birthright, baby. Your inheritance."

Over the following months, Jasmine became obsessed with family history. She interviewed every relative she could find. She visited the library to research census records and historical documents. She joined an online genealogy group.

She discovered relatives she'd never known existed. Stories that had been lost. Connections that went back centuries.

But more than facts, she discovered identity. Pride. A sense of belonging to something larger than herself.

At school, she started noticing when people dismissed their elders. When they treated older generations like they were obsolete, irrelevant, out of touch.

One day in the cafeteria, a girl was complaining about having to visit her grandmother.

"She just talks about the past constantly. It's so boring."

Jasmine spoke up. "Maybe she's trying to give you something valuable. Maybe those stories are her legacy to you."

"Stories about stuff that happened before I was born? How is that valuable?"

"Because that's where you came from. Those stories explain who you are. They connect you to something bigger than just your individual life." Jasmine thought about her own grandmother. "Trust me. Ask the questions. Listen to the stories. Someday those people won't be around anymore, and you'll wish you had."

For Mother's Day, Jasmine surprised her grandmother with a gift. A leather-bound journal filled with all the stories Grandma Rose had told her, transcribed and organized chronologically. Photos printed and carefully arranged. A family tree traced back as far as Jasmine could research.

"This is your legacy," Jasmine told her. "But it's also mine. And it'll be my children's and their children's. You gave me the gift of knowing where I come from. Now I'm preserving it so it never gets lost."

Grandma Rose held the journal like it was made of gold. "This is the most precious thing anyone has ever given me."

"It's the most precious thing you've ever given me," Jasmine replied. "I just finally learned to recognize its value."

At the end of the school year, Mr. Jackson asked Jasmine to speak at an assembly about her heritage project.

Standing in front of the entire school, Jasmine felt nervous but also proud.

"I used to think my family's history was boring," she began. "Old stories from old people that had nothing to do with my life. But I was wrong. My family's history is my history. Their struggles are the reason I have opportunities. Their strength is the foundation I'm building my life on.

I'm not just a teenage girl living in Chicago in 2025. I'm the descendant of enslaved people who survived unimaginable cruelty. The descendant of Civil Rights activists who risked everything for justice. The descendant of ordinary people who did extraordinary things.

And so are all of you. Every single person in this room comes from somewhere. Comes from someone. Has a history that explains who they are and why they matter.

Our elders aren't just old people telling boring stories. They're living libraries. Walking history books. The keepers of our identities and our inheritances.

So ask the questions. Listen to the stories. Learn your roots. Because they're not just history. They're treasure. Hidden treasure that's yours for the taking, if only you're willing to dig."

The auditorium erupted in applause.

That night, Jasmine sat with her grandmother on the porch, watching the sunset.

"You know what I realized?" Jasmine said. "All those times you were telling me stories and I was tuning you out? You weren't boring. I was just too young and self-centered to understand what you were offering me."

"You weren't ready yet," Grandma Rose said gently. "But you're ready now. And that's what matters."

"I'm sorry it took me so long."

"Don't be sorry, baby. Just keep listening. Keep learning. Keep honoring where you come from by living fully where you're going."

Jasmine leaned her head on her grandmother's shoulder, feeling connected to something vast and powerful. A lineage of strength. A legacy of resilience. Roots that ran deep and wide, anchoring her to the past while giving her wings to fly into the future.

"Thank you, Grandma," she whispered. "For not giving up on me. For keeping the stories alive until I was ready to hear them."

"That's what we do, baby. We pass the torch. Generation to generation. And now it's burning bright in you."

Jasmine smiled, feeling the weight and the gift of her inheritance. Her family's roots were indeed hidden treasure. And she was rich beyond measure.

Reflect & Grow

Questions for you:

- What do you know about your family history? Have you asked your elders about their lives and experiences?
- What stories from your family have been passed down? What do they tell you about who you are?
- If you could ask your grandparents or great-grandparents anything, what would it be?
- How does knowing where you come from change how you see yourself and your place in the world?

Remember: You are not self-made. You stand on the shoulders of everyone who came before you. Their struggles, their triumphs, their choices, they all led to you. Your family's history isn't just dusty old stories. It's your origin story. It explains your strength, your values, your identity. The elders in your life are living treasures, carrying memories and wisdom that will be lost when they're gone. Ask the questions now. Listen to the stories while you still can. Learn your roots. Because knowing where you came from helps you understand where you're going. And that knowledge is priceless.

Your Inner Voice Always Knows the Truth

Emma Sullivan had a bad feeling about Ryan.

She couldn't explain it exactly. He was popular, good-looking, and everyone seemed to think he was great. When he asked her out, her friends squealed with excitement.

"Oh my God, Emma! Ryan Harris? He's like, the most wanted guy in school!"

"You're so lucky!"

"I can't believe he picked you!"

Emma smiled and nodded, but that quiet voice inside her whispered: Something's not right.

She ignored it. Pushed it down. Told herself she was being paranoid, overthinking, self-sabotaging. Everyone else thought Ryan was perfect. Who was she to disagree?

Their first date was fine. Nice restaurant, good conversation. Ryan was charming, attentive, said all the right things.

But when he drove her home, he tried to kiss her and she pulled back instinctively.

"What's wrong?" Ryan asked, looking confused.

"Nothing. I just... I'm not ready for that yet."

"Come on, Emma. It's just a kiss. Don't be so uptight."

That word. Uptight. It stung. Made her feel like she was being unreasonable, immature, prudish.

"I'm sorry," Emma heard herself say. "You're right. I'm being silly."

She let him kiss her. It felt wrong. Forced. But she told herself that's just how first kisses are sometimes.

The voice inside her whispered: This isn't right. Listen to me.

She didn't listen.

Over the next few weeks, the bad feeling grew stronger. Little things that individually seemed minor but together formed a pattern.

Ryan always wanted to know where she was, who she was with, what she was doing. He got annoyed when she hung out with her friends instead of him. He made comments about her clothes, suggesting she wear things that were "more flattering."

Emma's best friend, Chloe, noticed.

"He seems kind of controlling," Chloe said carefully. "The way he keeps texting you constantly, getting mad when you don't respond immediately."

"He just likes me a lot," Emma defended. "He wants to spend time with me."

"But you look stressed all the time now. You're constantly checking your phone, worried about making him mad."

"I'm fine," Emma insisted. But she wasn't fine. She was exhausted, anxious, second-guessing everything she did.

The voice inside her was screaming now: Get out. This isn't love. This is control.

But Emma's rational mind overruled it. Ryan hadn't done anything obviously wrong. He hadn't hit her or called her names. He was just... intense. Passionate. That's what her friends called it. Passionate.

So why did it feel like drowning?

One Friday night, Emma told Ryan she wanted to go to her friend's birthday party.

"Without me?" Ryan's voice was cold over the phone.

"You weren't invited. It's just close friends."

"So I'm not close to you?"

"That's not what I meant. It's just..."

"You know what, Emma? Go to your stupid party. But don't expect me to be waiting around when you decide you have time for me."

He hung up.

Emma stared at her phone, her heart racing. That feeling in her gut was alarm bells now, sirens, red flags waving frantically.

Leave him, the voice said. You know this isn't right.

But the louder voice, the voice of doubt and fear and what everyone else thought, said: You're overreacting. He's just upset. You should apologize. You should make this work.

Emma texted: I'm sorry. I won't go to the party. I'll spend the evening with you instead.

The moment she hit send, she felt sick.

At school on Monday, Emma's English teacher, Mrs. Rodriguez, asked her to stay after class.

"Emma, I'm worried about you. Your grades have been slipping. You seem distracted. Is everything okay?"

"Everything's fine," Emma said automatically.

Mrs. Rodriguez looked at her for a long moment. "You know, when I was your age, I dated someone who made me feel small. Who made me question my own judgment constantly. Who isolated me from my friends and made me feel like I was always doing something wrong."

Emma's throat tightened.

"I ignored my gut feeling about him for a whole year," Mrs. Rodriguez continued. "Because everyone else thought he was great. Because I thought I was being dramatic. But you know what? That feeling in my gut? It was right all along. It was trying to protect me."

"How did you finally listen to it?"

"I realized that my inner voice knew the truth before my logical mind was ready to accept it. Our intuition is powerful, Emma. It picks up on patterns and red flags that our conscious mind wants to rationalize away. When something feels wrong, it usually is wrong."

That night, Emma lay in bed, finally allowing herself to really listen to that inner voice she'd been silencing for weeks.

What was it trying to tell her?

That Ryan made her feel anxious, not happy. That she was walking on eggshells, constantly worried about his reactions. That she'd stopped hanging out with her friends, stopped doing things she loved, shrunk herself to fit into the space he allowed her.

That this wasn't what love should feel like.

Her phone buzzed. A text from Ryan: Where are you? Why haven't you responded? Are you with someone else?

She'd been in the bathroom for five minutes.

Emma felt the fear and anxiety spike. Her first instinct was to text back immediately, to reassure him, to explain, to apologize for taking too long.

But another part of her, that quiet voice that had been trying to get her attention for weeks, said: You don't owe him constant access to you. This isn't normal. This is wrong.

For the first time, Emma listened.

She didn't text back immediately. She sat with the discomfort, with the anxiety, with the fear of his reaction.

And slowly, underneath all that fear, she found something else. Certainty. Clarity.

Her inner voice was right. It had been right all along.

The next day, Emma asked Ryan to meet her at a coffee shop. A public place. She'd learned that much from the domestic violence awareness assembly at school.

"We need to talk," Emma said.

"About what?" Ryan looked annoyed already.

"About us. About how this relationship makes me feel."

"Here we go. You're going to be dramatic again."

That word. Dramatic. Like her feelings weren't valid. Like her perspective didn't matter.

"I'm not being dramatic," Emma said, her voice steadier than she felt. "I'm being honest. This relationship doesn't feel right to me. I'm constantly anxious. I'm always worried about making you mad. I've stopped seeing my friends, stopped doing things I love. This isn't healthy."

"So now I'm the bad guy? I care about you, Emma. I want to spend time with you. If that's a crime, then I guess I'm guilty."

"Caring about someone shouldn't feel like control. Love shouldn't feel like walking on eggshells."

"You're being ridiculous. You're throwing away a great relationship because you're insecure and paranoid."

Emma felt the old doubt creeping in. Was she being ridiculous? Was she sabotaging something good?

But then she remembered Mrs. Rodriguez's words. Her inner voice knew the truth.

And the truth was: this relationship made her feel small, anxious, and trapped. That wasn't love.

"I'm not ridiculous," Emma said firmly. "I'm listening to my gut. And my gut says this isn't right for me. We're done, Ryan."

"You're making a huge mistake."

"Maybe. But it's my mistake to make."

Emma stood up and walked out, her heart pounding, her hands shaking. But underneath the fear was something stronger. Relief. Freedom. The rightness of finally listening to that inner voice.

The next few days were hard. Ryan tried to win her back with apologies and promises. Her friends, the ones who'd thought he was so great, didn't understand.

"He's so nice though! He really likes you!"

"You're being too picky."

"You'll regret this."

But Emma held firm. Because that inner voice, now that she was finally listening to it, was crystal clear.

And then other voices started joining in. Girls who'd dated Ryan before. Girls who had similar stories of feeling controlled, anxious, diminished.

"I'm so glad you got out," one girl told Emma. "I dated him for six months and it completely destroyed my self-esteem. But everyone kept telling me I was lucky to have him, so I thought I was crazy."

"You're not crazy," Emma said. "Your gut was right. We all need to start trusting ourselves more."

In the weeks after the breakup, Emma noticed something interesting. She felt lighter. Happier. Like she could breathe fully for the first time in months.

She reconnected with friends she'd been neglecting. She joined the photography club she'd been interested in. She did things simply because she wanted to, without worrying about someone else's reaction.

And most importantly, she started tuning in to that inner voice. Really listening to it.

When someone made her uncomfortable, she listened.

When an opportunity felt right, even if it scared her, she listened.

When something seemed too good to be true, she listened.

Her intuition, she realized, was like a compass. It didn't always tell her exactly where to go, but it always told her when she was heading in the wrong direction.

Months later, Emma was asked to speak at a school assembly about healthy relationships.

Standing in front of her peers, she felt nervous but also certain. This message mattered.

"I want to talk about something that saved me," Emma began. "Your inner voice. Your gut feeling. Your intuition. Whatever you want to call it.

We're constantly told to be logical, to ignore our feelings, to give people the benefit of the doubt. And those things have their place. But we're not taught to listen to that quiet voice inside us that knows when something isn't right.

I dated someone who everyone else thought was great. My friends loved him. He seemed perfect on paper. But something inside me knew it wasn't right. And I ignored that voice. For weeks, I told myself I was being paranoid, dramatic, overthinking.

But that voice was right. It was trying to protect me from a relationship that was slowly eroding my sense of self.

Your inner voice isn't being dramatic. It's not being paranoid. It's picking up on patterns and signals that your conscious mind wants to rationalize away. When something feels wrong, it usually is wrong. When someone makes you uncomfortable, even if you can't explain why, that matters. When you feel like you're losing yourself in a relationship, friendship, or situation, pay attention.

Your intuition is a gift. A superpower. A survival tool. Don't ignore it. Don't let other people's opinions drown it out. Don't rationalize it away.

Listen to it. Trust it. It knows the truth before your logical mind is ready to accept it."

The auditorium was silent. Then someone started clapping. Then another. Until the whole school was applauding.

After the assembly, dozens of students approached Emma. Many shared their own stories of ignoring their intuition and regretting it. Others thanked her for giving them permission to trust themselves.

That night, Emma wrote in her journal:

"I used to think being smart meant using only logic and reason. Ignoring feelings. Overriding gut instincts with rational thought.

But I've learned that true wisdom comes from integrating both. Logic and intuition. Reason and feeling. Head and gut.

My inner voice tried to warn me about Ryan from day one. But I didn't listen. I let other people's opinions and my own fears drown it out.

Never again.

Now I know: my inner voice is not my enemy. It's my most trusted ally. It knows things my conscious mind hasn't figured out yet. It sees patterns I'm not ready to acknowledge. It protects me from situations and people who aren't good for me.

Listening to it isn't being dramatic or paranoid. It's being wise. It's honoring the part of me that knows truth at a deeper level than words can express.

From now on, I'm tuning in. I'm listening. I'm trusting.

Because my inner voice always knows the truth. Even when I'm not ready to hear it."

Reflect & Grow

Questions for you:

- Can you remember a time when your gut feeling told you something was wrong, but you ignored it? What happened?
- What does your inner voice sound like? How do you distinguish it from fear or anxiety?
- Are there situations in your life right now where your intuition is trying to tell you something? Are you listening?
- What stops you from trusting your gut? Other people's opinions? Fear of being wrong? Wanting to be "nice"?

Remember: Your intuition is not your enemy. It's your internal guidance system, honed by evolution to keep you safe and help you thrive. When something feels wrong, even if you can't explain why, pay attention. Your gut picks up on patterns, inconsistencies, and red flags that your logical mind wants to explain away. Trusting yourself doesn't mean never doubting. It means giving weight to that inner knowing, especially when it's warning you away from something. You are allowed to leave situations that feel wrong, even if you can't fully articulate why. You are allowed to trust yourself more than you trust what others think you should do. Your inner voice knows the truth. Listen to it.

Someone Else's Success Isn't Your Failure

Taylor Bennett and her twin sister Morgan were born three minutes apart.

Those three minutes had defined their entire lives.

Morgan came first. Morgan walked first. Morgan talked first. Morgan was better at everything, first at everything, the star of everything.

And Taylor? Taylor was second. Always second. The other twin. Morgan's shadow.

When they were younger, it didn't bother Taylor as much. They were a team, two halves of a whole. But somewhere around middle school, things shifted. Morgan started pulling ahead, and Taylor started falling behind.

Or at least, that's how it felt.

Senior year was supposed to be Taylor's year. Her chance to finally step out of Morgan's shadow and be her own person.

Instead, it was more of the same.

Morgan made varsity soccer captain. Taylor made the team but rarely played.

Morgan got the lead in the school musical. Taylor was in the ensemble.

Morgan was nominated for homecoming queen. Taylor wasn't even on the ballot.

"It's like the universe has decided she gets everything and I get the leftovers," Taylor complained to her best friend Aiden.

"You're being dramatic," Aiden said, but not unkindly. "You have your own strengths. You're an incredible artist. Morgan can't draw to save her life."

"Nobody cares about art," Taylor muttered. "Not like they care about soccer and theater and homecoming."

What Taylor didn't say out loud was the darker thought underneath. If Morgan is successful, what does that make me? If she's the star, am I the failure?

The breaking point came when college acceptance letters started arriving.

Morgan got into Stanford. Early admission. Full scholarship.

The whole family celebrated. There was cake, champagne for the parents, endless congratulations. Morgan's face was radiant with pride and excitement.

Taylor smiled and hugged her sister and said all the right things. But inside, something was crumbling.

If Morgan got into Stanford, one of the best schools in the country, what did that say about Taylor? She'd applied to good schools too, but none as prestigious. And she hadn't heard back yet.

What if she didn't get in anywhere? What if Morgan went to Stanford and Taylor ended up at community college?

The three-minute gap would become a chasm.

That night, Taylor couldn't sleep. She lay in bed, spiraling into dark thoughts.

Morgan's success felt like Taylor's failure. Like there was only so much success to go around, and Morgan had taken it all, leaving nothing for Taylor.

It wasn't fair. It wasn't rational. But it's how she felt.

The next morning, Taylor was quiet at breakfast. Morgan, still glowing from her Stanford acceptance, didn't seem to notice.

"I can't believe it's really happening," Morgan said, scrolling through the Stanford website on her phone. "I'm going to California!"

"That's great," Taylor said flatly.

"You okay, Taylor?" her dad asked, noticing her mood.

"I'm fine."

But she wasn't fine. She was drowning in envy and self-pity and the awful, shameful feeling that her twin's success somehow diminished her own worth.

At school, everyone was talking about Morgan's Stanford acceptance. Teachers congratulated her in the hallways. Students high-fived her at lunch. The principal mentioned it in the morning announcements.

Taylor felt invisible. Or worse, visible only as Morgan's twin. The one who wasn't going to Stanford.

In art class, her favorite teacher, Ms. Reeves, noticed Taylor's distraction.

"You've been staring at that blank canvas for twenty minutes," Ms. Reeves said gently. "Want to talk about what's on your mind?"

"It's stupid."

"Try me."

Taylor set down her brush. "My sister got into Stanford. And I'm happy for her. I really am. But I also feel like her success makes me look like a failure. Like if she's the successful one, I must be the unsuccessful one."

Ms. Reeves was quiet for a moment. Then she said, "Can I tell you about my sister?"

Taylor nodded.

"My sister is a neurosurgeon. Brilliant, successful, saves lives daily. When we were growing up, she was the smart one, the driven one, the one everyone predicted would do amazing things. And me? I was the artsy one, the dreamer, the one who people worried about."

"But you're a great teacher," Taylor said.

"I know that now. But for a long time, I measured my worth against her achievements. She became a doctor, so I felt like a failure for becoming a teacher. She bought a house, so my apartment felt inadequate. She got married, so my singleness felt like something missing."

"What changed?"

"I realized I was playing a game I could never win. Because I was measuring my success using her yardstick, not mine. Her success didn't take anything away from me. There isn't a finite amount of success in the world where if she gets some, I get less. Success isn't a pie. It's infinite."

Taylor absorbed this. "But people compare us constantly. Twins get compared even more than regular siblings."

"People will compare. But you don't have to participate in that comparison. You don't have to accept their narrative that one of you is the successful one and one is the failure. You can write your own story."

That afternoon, Taylor went to the library to work on her art portfolio. She was applying to several art schools, places that valued creativity over test scores, that cared about vision more than GPA.

Looking through her work, Taylor felt something shift. These paintings, these drawings, they were good. Really good. They were hers in a way that nothing else was. Morgan couldn't do this. Nobody else could do this exactly like Taylor did it.

Why had she been dismissing her own talent just because it wasn't the same as Morgan's?

Her phone buzzed. A text from Morgan: Where are you? Want to grab dinner?

Taylor hesitated. Part of her wanted to avoid Morgan, to nurse her envy in private. But another part of her, a braver part, wanted to try something different.

She texted back: Library. Come find me?

When Morgan arrived, she found Taylor surrounded by her artwork.

"Wow," Morgan said, picking up a painting. "Taylor, this is incredible. I didn't know you were working on all this."

"It's my portfolio. For art school applications."

"You're going to get in everywhere. These are amazing." Morgan looked genuinely impressed. "I can't believe we're twins and you got all the artistic talent. So unfair."

Taylor looked at her sister. "What do you mean unfair? You got into Stanford."

"Yeah, but I can't create anything like this. All I can do is kick a ball and memorize lines." Morgan sat down. "You know what I'm jealous of? That you have this passion, this talent, this thing that's completely yours. Soccer is fun, but it's not who I am the way art is who you are."

Taylor stared at her sister. "You're jealous of me?"

"Of course. You're so talented, so creative, so unique. I'm just good at the things everyone values. But you're good at something that actually matters, something that will last."

It had never occurred to Taylor that Morgan might feel inadequate too. That comparison went both ways. That maybe they were both measuring themselves against each other and both coming up short.

"I've been so jealous of your Stanford acceptance," Taylor admitted. "I felt like your success made me a failure."

"Taylor, no. My getting into Stanford has nothing to do with you. We're on totally different paths. We always have been."

"But people compare us."

"So? Let them compare. It doesn't change the truth, which is that you're incredible in your own right. Not as my twin. As Taylor." Morgan squeezed her hand. "I'm sorry if I've ever made you feel less than. That was never my intention."

"It's not your fault. It's my own insecurity." Taylor felt tears prick her eyes. "I've been so focused on what you have that I haven't appreciated what I have."

Over the next few weeks, Taylor worked on shifting her mindset. It wasn't easy. Years of comparison couldn't be undone overnight.

But she started celebrating Morgan's wins without feeling like they diminished her own. When Morgan scored the winning goal at the championship game, Taylor cheered loudly from the stands. When Morgan got another scholarship offer, Taylor was genuinely happy for her.

And something surprising happened. The more Taylor celebrated Morgan's success, the less threatened she felt by it. It was like by releasing the envy, she made room for her own joy.

In March, Taylor's acceptance letters started arriving. She got into three art schools, including her top choice, the Rhode Island School of Design.

When she told her family, Morgan screamed with excitement and pulled her into a crushing hug.

"I knew it! I knew you'd get in! You're going to be a famous artist someday and I'll brag that you're my sister."

"You're going to Stanford and I'm going to RISD," Taylor said, the reality sinking in. "We're both going to be okay."

"We're both going to be better than okay," Morgan corrected. "We're going to be amazing. In completely different ways."

At graduation, Taylor gave a speech as valedictorian of the arts program. Morgan gave a speech as captain of the soccer team. Both speeches were different, both were excellent, both were celebrated.

Standing on stage, Taylor looked out at the crowd and realized something profound. Her worth wasn't determined by how she compared to Morgan. It never had been. She was valuable on her own terms, for her own gifts, in her own right.

"I spent a lot of my life feeling like I was in someone's shadow," Taylor said in her speech. "Comparing myself to people who seemed more successful, more talented, more everything. But I've learned something important. Someone else's success is not my failure. Their light doesn't dim mine. There's room for all of us to shine.

We're taught that life is a competition, that there are winners and losers, that someone else succeeding means we're failing. But that's not true. Success isn't finite. There's enough for everyone. Your classmate getting into a good college doesn't close the door on your dreams. Your friend's talent doesn't make yours less valuable. Your sibling's achievements don't define your worth.

We can celebrate each other's wins without feeling diminished by them. We can support each other's journeys without comparing our chapter one to someone else's chapter twenty. We can be happy for others and happy for ourselves at the same time.

So here's my challenge to all of us as we graduate. Stop measuring your worth against other people's achievements. Stop treating life like a competition where someone else's success is your failure. Start celebrating others genuinely, knowing it takes nothing away from you. Start focusing on your own path, your own gifts, your own timeline.

Because the truth is, there's enough success, enough happiness, enough opportunity for all of us. We just have to stop believing that someone else getting theirs means we can't have ours."

The auditorium erupted in applause. Morgan was in the front row, crying and clapping louder than anyone.

That night, Taylor and Morgan sat on the roof of their house like they used to when they were kids, looking at the stars.

"I'm going to miss you," Morgan said. "California is so far from Rhode Island."

"I'll miss you too. But I think the distance will be good for us. We'll both get to be our own people, not just 'the twins.'"

"We've always been our own people. We just forgot that for a while."

Taylor smiled. "You're right. And hey, we can FaceTime. Visit during breaks. It'll be fine."

"Better than fine," Morgan said. "We're both going to live amazing lives. Different lives, but equally amazing."

"To different but equally amazing," Taylor said, raising an imaginary glass.

"To success that multiplies instead of divides," Morgan added.

They clinked their imaginary glasses together and laughed, two sisters who'd finally learned that there was room for both of them to shine.

Three minutes apart didn't define them anymore. Their own unique paths did.

And that made all the difference.

Reflect & Grow

Questions for you:

- Have you ever felt like someone else's success was your failure? What was that like?
- Who do you compare yourself to most? Why do you think that is?
- Can you think of a time when you genuinely celebrated someone else's win? How did that feel?
- What would change if you believed there was enough success for everyone, including you?

Remember: Success is not a finite resource. Someone else achieving their dreams doesn't use up the success that was meant for you. Their light doesn't dim yours. Their win doesn't create your loss. You are on your own unique path, with your own timeline, your own gifts, your own definition of success. Comparing your beginning to someone else's middle or end is unfair to yourself. Measuring your worth against someone else's achievements misses the point entirely. You are not in competition with anyone except who you were yesterday. Celebrate others genuinely. Support their wins. And trust that there's plenty of room for you to succeed too, in your own way, in your own time.

Small Choices Build Your Big Future

Kayla Morrison didn't think much about her choices.

She hit snooze three times every morning. She scrolled through TikTok during class. She put off homework until the last minute. She ate whatever was convenient. She skipped workouts when she didn't feel like it.

They were just small things. Tiny decisions that didn't really matter in the grand scheme of things.

Or so she thought.

"Kayla, we need to talk about your grades," her mom said, holding up a progress report. Three C's, two D's, and an F in chemistry.

"It's not my fault. The teachers are boring. The homework is stupid. I'll do better next semester."

"You said that last semester. And the semester before that." Her mom looked worried, not angry. "Honey, you're a junior. Colleges are going to look at these grades. You're running out of time to turn this around."

"I know, I know. I'll try harder."

But Kayla didn't try harder. She made the same choices she always made. Hit snooze. Scrolled during class. Procrastinated on homework.

They were just small choices. How much could they really matter?

In health class, Mr. Patterson started a unit on decision-making.

"Every choice you make, no matter how small, is a vote for the kind of person you want to become," he said, writing on the board. "You don't become successful with one big decision. You become successful with a thousand small decisions made consistently over time."

Kayla rolled her eyes. Here we go with another boring lecture about responsibility.

But Mr. Patterson continued. "Think of it like this. Every time you hit snooze, you're voting for the person who values sleep more than punctuality. Every time you choose to scroll instead of study, you're voting for the person who prioritizes distraction over achievement. Every choice is a vote. What are you voting for?"

The question stuck with Kayla more than she wanted to admit.

That weekend, Kayla's older cousin Nicole came to visit. Nicole was in her second year at Georgetown, studying international relations, living the life Kayla dreamed of.

"How did you get into Georgetown?" Kayla asked. "Your high school grades weren't that great either, right?"

"They were okay by senior year. But freshman and sophomore year? I was a lot like you. Lazy, unmotivated, coasting." Nicole sat on Kayla's bed. "What changed was I realized that the person I was being every day wasn't the person I wanted to become."

"What do you mean?"

"I wanted to be successful, go to a good college, have options. But my daily choices were voting for someone completely different. Someone who didn't care, who took the easy route, who prioritized short-term comfort over long-term goals."

"So what did you do?"

"I started small. Really small. I made my bed every morning. Sounds stupid, right? But it was one small choice that said 'I'm the kind of person who does what they say they'll do.' Then I added another small choice. I'd review my notes for ten minutes before bed. Just ten minutes. Then I started waking up on the first alarm. Small choices, consistently made, that added up to becoming a different person."

Kayla thought about this. "But how do small things like making your bed matter for college?"

"They don't, directly. But they build discipline. They build self-trust. They build the muscle of following through on commitments. And that muscle is what got me through organic chemistry and eighteen-page research papers and everything else that was hard."

Monday morning, Kayla's alarm went off. Her hand reached for the snooze button automatically.

Then she remembered Nicole's words. Every choice is a vote.

Hitting snooze was a vote for the person who prioritized ten more minutes of sleep over being the kind of person who does what they say they'll do.

Kayla's finger hovered over the snooze button. Then she forced herself to sit up and turn off the alarm.

It was just one small choice. But it felt significant.

She made her bed. Another small choice. Two minutes that didn't matter except that they did.

At breakfast, her mom looked surprised to see her on time and dressed.

"Everything okay?" her mom asked.

"Yeah. Just trying something different."

In first period, Kayla's phone buzzed with a TikTok notification. Normally, she'd check it immediately, spend ten minutes scrolling, miss half the lesson.

Every choice is a vote.

Kayla put her phone in her backpack and actually listened to the teacher. She took notes. She asked a question when she didn't understand something.

Small choices. But each one was a vote for the person she wanted to become.

It wasn't easy. Every day, Kayla faced a hundred small choices. And every day, she wanted to take the easy route, the familiar route, the route she'd always taken.

But she kept hearing Mr. Patterson's voice. Every choice is a vote.

So she voted. Again and again.

Wake up on the first alarm. Make the bed. Review notes before class. Actually do the homework instead of copying someone else's. Go to the library instead of scrolling on her phone. Choose an apple instead of chips. Do ten push-ups before bed.

Tiny choices. None of them felt particularly important in the moment.

But after two weeks, Kayla noticed something. Her chemistry grade had gone from an F to a D+. Not great, but improvement.

After a month, she'd lost three pounds without really trying. Just from the accumulated effect of choosing slightly healthier options.

After six weeks, she realized she'd been on time to every single class. No tardies. No rushing. No stress.

Small choices, accumulated over time, were building something.

Her friend Bree noticed the changes.

"You're being really weird lately," Bree said at lunch. "What's going on?"

"What do you mean?"

"You're like, actually paying attention in class. You're not on your phone constantly. You seem different."

"I'm just trying to make better choices."

Bree laughed. "Okay, but why? Senior year is supposed to be fun. Why are you suddenly acting all responsible?"

"Because I want to go to a good college. And the version of me who was hitting snooze and scrolling through class wasn't going to get there."

"One semester of trying hard won't fix your transcript."

"Maybe not. But one semester of small choices, made consistently, will start building the person who can get there." Kayla surprised herself with how certain she sounded. "I spent three years voting for the wrong person. I'm changing my vote."

It wasn't always linear. Some days, Kayla fell back into old patterns. She'd hit snooze, skip homework, waste time on her phone.

But the difference was, now she noticed. And she could course-correct.

One bad choice didn't erase all the good ones. The key was the overall direction, the accumulated effect of voting for the right person more often than not.

By the end of the semester, Kayla's grades had improved dramatically. Three B's, two C's, and a C- in chemistry. Still not perfect, but a massive improvement from three C's, two D's and an F.

More importantly, Kayla felt different. Stronger. More capable. Like she was finally becoming the person she'd always wanted to be.

In the spring, college applications loomed. Kayla's GPA was better but still not great. Her test scores were average. On paper, she wasn't a standout candidate.

But for her college essay, Kayla wrote about transformation. About the power of small choices. About learning that who you become isn't determined by one big decision but by a thousand small ones, made consistently over time.

She wrote about hitting snooze and what that choice represented. About making her bed and building self-trust. About the discipline muscle and how it develops through small, daily practice.

"Your future isn't built in moments of big inspiration," she wrote. "It's built in the mundane moments of daily choice. Do you get up or hit snooze? Do you study or scroll? Do you choose the easy thing or the right thing? These tiny choices seem insignificant in the moment. But accumulated over time, they become your life."

Her English teacher, reading the draft, had tears in her eyes.

"This is powerful, Kayla. This is the best writing I've seen from you in three years."

"Thanks. It's true, too. I learned it the hard way."

Kayla got accepted to three colleges. Not Georgetown like Nicole, but good schools where she could build on the foundation she'd started.

The day she got her acceptance letter to State University, she called Nicole.

"I got in!"

"Kayla, that's amazing! I'm so proud of you!"

"I couldn't have done it without your advice. That conversation we had about small choices changed everything."

"You did the hard part. I just planted the seed. You're the one who watered it every single day with your choices."

"I'm nervous though. What if I fall back into old habits in college?"

"You might, sometimes. But you've built the muscle now. You know how to course-correct. You know that every choice is a vote. Just keep voting for the person you want to become."

At graduation, Kayla was asked to speak as part of a panel on "Lessons Learned."

Standing in front of her classmates, she felt nervous but ready.

"Three years ago, I was failing chemistry and coasting through life on autopilot," Kayla began. "I made choices without thinking about them. Hit snooze, scroll through class, procrastinate on homework. They seemed like small, insignificant decisions.

But those small decisions were building my life. They were voting for the kind of person I was becoming. And the person I was becoming wasn't someone I was proud of.

Someone told me that every choice is a vote for the kind of person you want to be. And I realized I'd been voting wrong. So I started voting differently.

I woke up on the first alarm. I made my bed. I paid attention in class. I did my homework on time. Tiny choices that felt almost silly in their smallness.

But those tiny choices accumulated. They built on each other. They created momentum. And slowly, they transformed not just my grades but who I was as a person.

I learned that you don't become successful with one big decision. You become successful with a thousand small decisions, made consistently, over time. You build your future one choice at a time.

So my challenge to all of you is this: look at your daily choices. Your autopilot decisions. The things you do without thinking. Are those choices voting for the person you want to become? Or are they voting for someone else entirely?

You have more control over your future than you think. Not through one big dramatic change, but through small, consistent choices. Every single day, you get to vote. Make sure you're voting for the right person."

The auditorium was silent. Then the applause started, growing louder and louder.

That night, Kayla wrote in her journal, a habit she'd developed as part of her small daily choices:

"A year ago, I didn't think small choices mattered. I thought big, dramatic decisions were what shaped your life.

But I've learned that big decisions are actually pretty rare. Most of life is lived in the small moments. The daily choices. The mundane decisions that don't feel important but actually are.

Do you get up or hit snooze? Do you show up or make excuses? Do you do the work or take the shortcut? Do you choose comfort or growth?

These tiny choices seem insignificant. But they're not. They're votes. And the accumulated votes determine who you become.

I'm not perfect. I still make bad choices sometimes. I still hit snooze occasionally, still procrastinate, still take the easy route.

But the difference is, now I'm conscious of it. Now I know that every choice matters. Now I understand that I'm building my future, one small decision at a time.

And that's empowering. Because it means I'm not at the mercy of one big break or one lucky opportunity. I'm in control, every single day, through the choices I make.

Small choices build big futures. I'm living proof of that.

And I'm excited to see what future I build, one choice at a time."

Reflect & Grow

Questions for you:

- What are your daily autopilot choices? The things you do without thinking? Are those choices voting for the person you want to become?
- If you could change one small habit that would compound over time, what would it be?
- Think about where you want to be in five years. What small daily choices would get you there?
- What's one tiny choice you could make tomorrow that would be a vote for your future self?

Remember: Your life isn't shaped by occasional big decisions. It's shaped by the accumulation of small choices made consistently over time. Every time you choose discipline over comfort, growth over ease, your future self over your present self, you're building something. It won't feel dramatic. It won't feel like you're changing the world. But those tiny choices compound. They accumulate. They become your life. You don't need to overhaul everything at once. You just need to make one small choice today that votes for the person you want to become. Then another tomorrow. And another the day after. Small choices, consistently made, build big futures. Start voting for yours.

Giving Enriches More Than Receiving

Ava Lawson had everything she wanted for her sixteenth birthday.

A new iPhone. Designer clothes. A promise of a car when she got her license. Her parents spared no expense, and Ava had learned to expect that. She was their only child, and they could afford to spoil her.

But as she sat surrounded by torn wrapping paper and expensive gifts, Ava felt something unexpected.

Empty.

"Don't you love everything?" her mom asked, noticing Ava's expression.

"Yeah, of course. Thank you." Ava forced a smile.

But the truth was, the gifts didn't excite her the way they used to. Getting more stuff just felt like getting more stuff. There was no joy in it anymore. No meaning.

Just more things to add to the pile of things she already had.

At school on Monday, Ava's friends gushed over her birthday haul.

"You're so lucky," Jessica said, admiring Ava's new designer purse. "Your parents are so generous."

"I wish my parents would buy me stuff like that," another friend added.

Ava smiled and accepted the compliments, but the emptiness remained. She had everything, but somehow it felt like nothing.

During lunch, she noticed a flyer on the bulletin board. "Winter Clothing Drive. Help families in need stay warm this season. Donations accepted in the main office."

Ava had seen these flyers before and never paid attention. But today, something made her pause.

Families in need. What did that even mean? Ava had never needed anything in her life.

That afternoon, Ava's community service coordinator, Mrs. Harper, stopped her in the hallway.

"Ava, you still need to complete your community service hours for graduation. You're quite behind."

"I know. I've been busy."

"I understand, but this isn't optional. You need twenty hours by the end of the semester." Mrs. Harper pulled out a list. "There are several opportunities. The food bank, the animal shelter, tutoring program..."

"Whatever's easiest," Ava said, not really caring.

"How about the community center? They run an after-school program for kids whose parents work late. They need volunteers to help with homework and activities."

"Sure, fine. Whatever."

Ava signed up, viewing it purely as a box to check. Get the hours, graduate, move on with her life.

She had no idea it would change everything.

The community center was in a part of town Ava rarely visited. The building was old, the paint was peeling, and the playground equipment looked like it had seen better days.

Inside, about fifteen kids ranging from ages six to twelve were doing homework at mismatched tables.

"You must be Ava," said Ms. Rodriguez, the program director. "Thanks for volunteering. We can use all the help we can get."

"No problem. What do you want me to do?"

"Just circulate, help with homework, play with the kids. Be present."

Be present. Ava could do that. For twenty hours, anyway.

She approached a table where a little girl was struggling with math homework, tears of frustration in her eyes.

"Hey, I'm Ava. Need help?"

The girl, whose name was Lily, looked up with big brown eyes. "I don't understand fractions. They're stupid."

Ava sat down. "They're not stupid. They're just confusing at first. Let me show you a trick."

For the next thirty minutes, Ava worked with Lily on fractions. And something strange happened. When Lily finally understood, when her face lit up with comprehension and pride, Ava felt something she hadn't felt in a long time.

Joy. Real, genuine joy.

Not from getting something, but from giving something.

Over the next few weeks, Ava kept coming back to the community center. Not because she had to, though she did need the hours. But because she wanted to.

She learned the kids' names, their stories, their struggles. Most came from low-income families. Some were in foster care. Many had parents working multiple jobs just to make ends meet.

These kids didn't have designer clothes or new iPhones or cars waiting for them. Some didn't even have warm winter coats.

But they had something Ava had been missing. They had resilience. Gratitude. They appreciated the smallest things. A new pencil. A snack. Someone taking time to help with homework.

One afternoon, a boy named Marcus showed Ava a drawing he'd made.

"This is my family," he said proudly, pointing to stick figures. "That's my mom, my two brothers, and me."

"It's beautiful. Where's your dad?"

"Don't have one. He left when I was little. But it's okay. My mom works really hard to take care of us."

Marcus said it so matter-of-factly, without self-pity. Like this was just his reality, and he was making the best of it.

Ava thought about her own complaints. About how she'd been feeling empty despite having everything. And she felt ashamed.

As Christmas approached, the community center was planning a holiday party for the kids.

"We're trying to get small gifts for each child," Ms. Rodriguez explained. "Nothing big, just something to make them feel special. But our budget is tight this year."

Ava thought about the pile of gifts from her birthday. The things she didn't really need or even want. The emptiness she'd felt despite the abundance.

"What if I organized a donation drive?" Ava said suddenly. "At my school. We could collect toys and clothes and supplies."

"That would be wonderful, but it's a lot of work."

"I want to do it."

Ava threw herself into the project. She made flyers, posted on social media, set up collection boxes around school. She talked to teachers, recruited friends, spread the word.

At first, people were skeptical. Ava Lawson, the girl who had everything, was running a charity drive?

But Ava's passion was genuine, and it showed. She talked about the kids at the community center, about their needs, about how a small gift could mean so much.

Slowly, donations started coming in. Toys, books, clothes, school supplies. Her classmates, many of whom came from privileged backgrounds like Ava, began to see beyond their own bubble.

Jessica donated a barely-used winter coat. "I have three others. Someone else needs this more than I do."

Other students followed. The collection boxes filled up.

Ava's parents watched this transformation with amazement.

"I'm proud of you, honey," her dad said one night. "This is really special, what you're doing."

"It feels good," Ava admitted. "Better than getting stuff for myself ever did."

The week before Christmas, Ava organized a wrapping party. She invited friends from school to the community center to wrap all the donated gifts.

"This is so much stuff," one friend marveled, looking at the piles of donations.

"And every single item is going to a kid who really needs it," Ava said. "That's what makes it meaningful."

They spent the afternoon wrapping, laughing, sharing stories about the donation drive. And Ava realized something. This felt more fulfilling than her own birthday party had. This sense of purpose, of making a difference, of giving instead of receiving.

This was what had been missing.

The day of the holiday party, Ava helped Ms. Rodriguez set up. They hung decorations, arranged gifts, prepared snacks. The community center looked transformed, festive and warm.

When the kids arrived, their faces lit up. Many had never had a party like this before.

Lily, the girl Ava had first helped with fractions, ran up and hugged her.

"Miss Ava! You're here!"

"Of course I'm here. I wouldn't miss this."

During the gift distribution, Ava watched as each child received their present. The joy on their faces, the genuine gratitude, the way they clutched their gifts like treasures.

Marcus got a basketball he'd been wanting. His eyes filled with tears.

"I can't believe this is mine," he whispered. "Thank you. Thank you so much."

Ava felt her own eyes water. She'd received dozens of gifts in her life and never felt what Marcus was feeling now. Because she'd never had to want for anything. She'd never experienced the gift of receiving something truly needed and appreciated.

But in giving, in being part of creating that joy, Ava felt something richer than any gift she'd ever received.

After the party, Ms. Rodriguez pulled Ava aside.

"You know, when you first started volunteering, I thought you were just here to check a box. Get your hours and leave."

"I was," Ava admitted.

"But you became something more. You became someone who truly cares. You've made a real difference in these kids' lives."

"They've made a difference in mine," Ava said. "I came here thinking I had everything. But I was wrong. I had stuff. I didn't have purpose. I didn't have meaning. These kids taught me what actually matters."

"What's that?"

"Connection. Making a difference. Being part of something bigger than yourself. Giving instead of just taking." Ava smiled. "I spent sixteen years thinking happiness came from getting what I wanted. But the happiest I've ever been is when I'm giving to others."

After completing her required hours, Ava kept volunteering. It became a regular part of her life, not an obligation but a choice.

She also changed other things. For Christmas, instead of asking for more stuff she didn't need, she asked her parents to donate to the community center in her name.

"Are you sure?" her mom asked. "Don't you want anything for yourself?"

"I have enough. More than enough. I'd rather help kids who don't."

Her parents looked at each other, then at their daughter, seeing the growth and maturity that had emerged.

"We're so proud of you," her dad said.

At school, Ava started a club called "Give Back." It organized regular volunteer opportunities and fundraisers for local charities.

"Our generation is really lucky," Ava told the club members at their first meeting. "Most of us have so much. But with that privilege comes responsibility. To give back. To help others. To use what we have to make a difference."

The club grew. Students who'd never thought about volunteering discovered the joy of giving. The school's culture began to shift, becoming more community-focused, less self-centered.

And it all started because Ava had felt empty despite having everything, and learned that giving fills you up in ways receiving never can.

For her college essays, Ava wrote about this transformation. About the emptiness of privilege without purpose. About learning that true wealth isn't measured in what you have, but in what you give.

"I used to measure my worth by what I owned," she wrote. "The brands I wore, the phone I carried, the gifts I received. But those things left me feeling hollow. It wasn't until I started giving, truly giving of my time and energy and care, that I felt rich. Because giving doesn't deplete you. It enriches you. It fills you with purpose and connection and joy that no material possession ever could."

Her English teacher called it the best essay she'd read in twenty years of teaching.

On Ava's seventeenth birthday, she did something different. Instead of a party with gifts, she organized a volunteer day. She invited her friends to spend the day at the community center, playing with kids, helping with homework, being present.

Some friends didn't understand. "Don't you want a real party? With gifts?"

"This is my real party," Ava said. "And these kids are my gift."

At the end of the day, surrounded by children she'd come to love, Ava felt something she hadn't felt at her sixteenth birthday party surrounded by expensive presents.

Fullness. Meaning. Purpose. Joy.

Lily hugged her tight. "This was the best day, Miss Ava."

"For me too, Lily. For me too."

Because Ava had learned the secret that took some people a lifetime to discover. That giving doesn't take from you. It adds to you. That generosity enriches the giver more than the receiver. That the path to true fulfillment isn't through getting more, but through giving more.

She'd spent sixteen years accumulating things, chasing happiness in possessions and privileges.

But it was in giving them away, in sharing, in serving, that she finally found what she'd been looking for all along.

Not emptiness, but fullness.

Not getting, but giving.

And that made all the difference.

Reflect & Grow

Questions for you:

- When was the last time you gave something without expecting anything in return? How did it feel?
- What do you have (time, talent, resources) that you could share with others?
- Think about the times you've felt most fulfilled. Were they when you received something or when you gave something?
- What's one way you could give back to your community this week?

Remember: True wealth isn't measured by what you have. It's measured by what you give. Generosity doesn't deplete you, it enriches you. When you give your time, your energy, your resources, your care, you receive something money can't buy: purpose, connection, meaning, joy. The more you give, the richer you become in the things that actually matter. You don't need to have a lot to give. You can give your time, your attention, your kindness. And in giving, you'll discover what so many before you have learned: that the path to true fulfillment isn't through getting more, but through giving more.

Your Values Are Your Compass

Sierra Jackson stood at a crossroads, literally and figuratively.

To her left was the party everyone was going to. The biggest party of the year, thrown by the most popular seniors. Everyone who was anyone would be there. Including Jake, the guy she'd been crushing on for months.

To her right was her little brother's championship basketball game. The one he'd been working toward all season. The one where he'd specifically asked Sierra to come because their parents had to work.

"Come on, Sierra," her friend Madison urged. "Your brother will understand. This party is legendary. You can't miss it."

"But I promised Malik I'd be there."

"He's ten. He'll get over it. Jake is going to be at the party. This is your chance!"

Sierra looked at her phone. A text from Malik: "Game starts in an hour. You're still coming, right?"

Her heart twisted. She knew what she wanted to do. She wanted to go to the party, to see Jake, to be part of the social scene.

But she also knew what she should do. What her values told her to do.

The problem was, Sierra wasn't entirely sure what her values were. She'd spent so long doing what everyone else wanted, what looked good, what was popular, that she'd never stopped to ask herself what actually mattered to her.

Sierra went to the party.

She told herself Malik would understand. That one game wasn't a big deal. That this opportunity with Jake was too important to miss.

But the whole night, she felt sick. Every time she laughed at a joke or danced or tried to talk to Jake, a voice inside her whispered: You're in the wrong place.

At 9 PM, her phone buzzed. A text from her mom: "Malik's team won! He scored the winning basket! Wish you could have been there."

Then a photo. Malik holding a trophy, smiling huge, his eyes scanning the crowd behind him. Looking for Sierra.

Sierra's stomach dropped. She'd missed it. She'd missed his moment because she chose a party over a promise. Because she chose what she wanted over what mattered.

She left the party early, Jake forgotten, feeling hollow and ashamed.

When Sierra got home, Malik was already in bed. She knocked softly on his door.

"Malik? You awake?"

"Yeah." His voice was flat.

Sierra sat on the edge of his bed. "I'm so sorry I missed your game. I heard you won. I heard you scored the winning basket."

"It's fine. Whatever."

"It's not fine. I promised I'd be there and I wasn't. I made a choice that went against what I know is right. And I'm really, truly sorry."

Malik was quiet for a moment. "Why did you go to the party instead?"

"Because I wanted to. Because it seemed important at the time. Because I was being selfish."

"Did you have fun at least?"

Sierra thought about it. "No. Not really. I felt wrong the whole time. Like I was in the wrong place."

"That's because you were," Malik said simply. "You were supposed to be at my game."

His words hit Sierra hard. He was right. Not just about the game, but about something bigger. She'd been in the wrong place because she'd acted against her values. And when you act against your values, nothing feels right, no matter how much you try to enjoy it.

The next morning, Sierra couldn't shake the guilty feeling. She'd let Malik down, yes. But more than that, she'd let herself down. She'd shown that her word didn't mean anything. That her promises were flexible. That popularity mattered more than integrity.

Is that who she wanted to be?

In her room, Sierra pulled out a notebook and started writing.

"What matters to me? What are my values?"

She stared at the blank page. It was harder than she expected. She'd spent so long caring about what other people thought, what looked good, what was popular, that she'd never defined her own values.

So she started simple. What made her feel good? What made her feel proud? What, when she did it, made her feel like herself?

Slowly, a list emerged:
- Keeping promises
- Being there for family
- Honesty
- Kindness
- Doing the right thing even when it's hard
- Integrity

Sierra looked at the list. These weren't flashy values. They weren't cool or trendy. But they were hers. Or at least, they were who she wanted to be.

And last night, she'd violated every single one of them.

At school on Monday, Madison grabbed Sierra's arm.

"Oh my God, you left the party so early! You totally missed it. Jake was asking about you!"

"Really?" Sierra felt a flutter of excitement, then remembered. The values list. The promise to Malik. The sick feeling of being in the wrong place.

"Yeah! You should text him. I think he likes you."

Sierra pulled out her phone, started to type a message to Jake, then stopped.

What did she actually know about Jake? That he was popular and good-looking. But what were his values? Did he keep his promises? Was he kind? Was he honest?

She didn't know. And more importantly, she realized she'd been so focused on whether Jake liked her that she'd never asked whether she actually liked him. Whether his values aligned with hers.

"Maybe," Sierra said to Madison. "I'll think about it."

That afternoon, Sierra had a meeting with her guidance counselor, Ms. Patterson, about college applications.

"So, Sierra, tell me about yourself. What's important to you? What are your values?"

There was that word again. Values.

"I'm actually figuring that out right now," Sierra admitted. "I made a mistake this weekend that made me realize I don't really know what I stand for. I've been so focused on fitting in and being liked that I never defined my own values."

Ms. Patterson nodded thoughtfully. "That's a very mature realization. Most people don't figure that out until much later. So what have you discovered?"

Sierra pulled out her list and read it to Ms. Patterson.

"Those are solid values," Ms. Patterson said. "Now the question is, are you living by them?"

"Not always. That's the problem. Like this weekend, I chose a party over my brother's game because I wanted to be popular. But my values say family and keeping promises matter. So I acted against my values and felt terrible."

"That's called cognitive dissonance. When your actions don't align with your values, you feel internal conflict. The solution isn't to change your values. It's to change your actions."

"But that's hard. Sometimes what my values say I should do isn't what I want to do."

"That's the definition of integrity," Ms. Patterson said. "Doing what's right even when it's hard. Using your values as a compass to guide your decisions, even when the path is difficult."

Sierra started using her values as a decision-making tool. Every time she faced a choice, she asked herself: What would the person with these values do?

When Madison invited her to copy homework, Sierra said no. Even though it was easier. Even though Madison got annoyed. Because honesty and integrity were her values.

When the popular girls started gossiping about someone, Sierra walked away. Even though it meant potentially being excluded. Because kindness was her value.

When her parents asked her to babysit Malik so they could go to a work event, she said yes. Even though her friends were going to the movies. Because family was her value.

It wasn't easy. Sometimes Sierra felt like she was missing out. Sometimes she worried she was becoming unpopular or boring.

But something interesting happened. The more she aligned her actions with her values, the better she felt. The internal conflict disappeared. She felt solid, grounded, sure of herself.

She felt like she knew who she was.

One Friday night, Sierra faced her biggest test yet.

There was a huge party, and Jake had specifically invited her. He'd texted: "Hope you can make it. Would love to hang out."

But that same night, Malik had a school project presentation he was nervous about. He'd asked Sierra to help him practice.

Party with Jake, or helping Malik. Want versus should.

Sierra looked at her values list, now taped to her mirror.

Family. Keeping promises. Doing the right thing even when it's hard.

The answer was clear.

She texted Jake: "Thanks for the invite, but I have a family commitment tonight. Maybe another time?"

Then she sat down with Malik and helped him practice his presentation until he felt confident and ready.

"Thanks, Sierra," Malik said when they finished. "You're a really good sister."

Those words meant more than any party ever could.

The next week, something unexpected happened. Jake approached Sierra at school.

"Hey, I got your text. Family commitment, huh?"

"Yeah, my little brother needed help with something."

Jake smiled. "That's cool. I respect that. Most people would have ditched their family for a party."

"I used to be one of those people. But I'm trying to be different now. Trying to live by my values."

"What are your values?" Jake asked, genuinely curious.

Sierra listed them. Family, integrity, honesty, kindness, keeping promises.

Jake nodded slowly. "I like that. You know what my biggest value is? Loyalty. I can't stand people who say one thing and do another. People whose words don't match their actions."

"So we have similar values," Sierra said, surprised.

"Yeah, we do. That's rare." Jake smiled. "Want to grab coffee sometime? Somewhere we can actually talk?"

Sierra felt butterflies, but different ones than before. Not nervous-excited butterflies about a popular boy. But genuine-connection butterflies about someone whose values aligned with hers.

"I'd like that," she said.

In her college essay, Sierra wrote about discovering her values and learning to use them as a compass.

"For most of my life, I navigated by other people's maps," she wrote. "I went where everyone else was going, did what everyone else was doing, valued what everyone else valued. I had no internal compass. No clear sense of who I was or what mattered to me.

Then I made a choice that violated my values, and I felt the dissonance. The internal conflict of knowing I'd done the wrong thing, even though it was the popular thing.

That's when I realized I needed to define my own values. To create my own compass. Because without knowing what matters to you, every decision is a struggle. Every choice feels arbitrary. You're just reacting to external pressures instead of acting from internal conviction.

But when you know your values, when you use them as a compass to guide your decisions, everything becomes clearer. Not easier, but clearer. You know what to do even when it's hard. You know who you are even when others disagree.

Your values are your compass. They point you toward the life you want to live, the person you want to become. And the more you follow that compass, even when the path is difficult, the more you become authentically, truly yourself."

Ms. Patterson called it the most mature and insightful essay she'd ever read from a high school student.

At graduation, Sierra was chosen to give one of the student speeches. Standing in front of her classmates, she felt nervous but grounded. She knew what she wanted to say.

"We're about to go out into the world and make a thousand choices," Sierra began. "Big choices about college and careers and relationships. Small choices about how we spend our time and who we spend it with.

Without a compass, those choices can feel overwhelming. How do you know what to do when everyone has different advice? When you want different things? When the easy path conflicts with the right path?

I learned this year that the compass you need is already inside you. It's your values. The things that matter to you at your core. Not what your parents value, or your friends value, or what society says you should value. Your values. The principles that define who you are and who you want to become.

When you know your values, decision-making becomes simpler. Not easier, but simpler. You ask yourself: which choice aligns with my values? Which path is true to who I am?

And then you follow that path, even when it's hard. Especially when it's hard. Because integrity means doing what's right according to your values, not what's easy or popular or convenient.

So my challenge to all of you is this: define your values. Write them down. Make them concrete. Then use them as your compass. Let them guide your choices, big and small. Let them show you who you are and who you're becoming.

Because when you live according to your values, when your actions align with your principles, you become unshakeable. You know who you are. And that knowledge, that internal compass, will guide you through every challenge and every opportunity that lies ahead.

Your values are your compass. Follow them home to yourself."

The auditorium erupted in applause. Sierra saw Malik in the crowd, clapping and smiling with pride. She saw her parents, tears in their eyes. She saw Ms. Patterson, nodding with approval.

And she saw Jake, who caught her eye and mouthed: "That was perfect."

Because it was true. Values weren't just abstract concepts. They were the compass that guided you through life, the North Star that showed you who you were meant to become.

And Sierra had finally found hers.

Reflect & Grow

Questions for you:

- What are your core values? If you're not sure, think about moments when you felt most proud or most disappointed in yourself. What values were honored or violated?
- Are your daily choices aligned with your values? Where is there disconnect?
- Think of a recent difficult decision. If you'd used your values as a compass, would you have chosen differently?
- What would change in your life if you let your values guide all your choices?

Remember: You will face thousands of choices in your life. Some will be easy, many will be hard. But when you know your values, when you've defined what matters to you at your core, every decision becomes clearer. Your values are your compass, pointing you toward the life you want to live and the person you want to become. Don't let other people's values guide your choices. Don't let external pressure override internal conviction. Define what matters to you, then have the courage to live by it. When your actions align with your values, when you follow your own compass, you become authentically, powerfully, beautifully yourself. And that's the ultimate success.

A Final Note

"Helping one person might not change the whole world, but it could change the world for one person."

Would you help a teenage girl you've never met if it took less than 60 seconds and cost you nothing? She's searching for stories that understand her struggles. She's trying to figure out who she is in a complicated world. And your honest review can help her find these stories.

The only way I can help teenage girls navigate their challenges is by reaching them first. And most people judge a book by its reviews.

If you found value in these stories, would you take a moment to leave an honest review?

Your review helps:

- One more girl feel less alone
- One more parent connect with their daughter
- One more life feel understood

Scan to leave a review

Thank you from the bottom of my heart.

Grace.

www.ingramcontent.com/pod-product-compliance
Lightning Source LLC
Chambersburg PA
CBHW060046230426
43661CB00004B/680